True Stories
2

Sandra Heyer

True Stories: Level 2, Silver Edition

Pearson Education, 221 River Street, Hoboken, NJ 07030

Staff Credits: The people who made up the *True Stories: Level 2, Silver Edition* team, representing content creation, design, manufacturing, marketing, multimedia, project management, publishing, rights management, and testing, are Pietro Alongi, Tracey Cataldo, Dave Dickey, Warren Fischbach, Lucy Hart, Gosia Jaros-White, Barry Katzen, Linda Moser, Dana Pinter, Paula Van Ells, Joseph Vella, and Peter West.

Text design and layout: Don Williams
Composition: Page Designs International
Project supervision: Bernard Seal
Contributing editor: Bernard Seal

Cover images: *(from top to bottom)* Aila Images/Shutterstock; Paul Wolf/123RF; Stephan Stockinger/123RF; wavebreakmedia/Shutterstock; Jakub Cejpek/Shutterstock; *(silver edition badge)* deepstock/Shutterstock.
Illustrations: Don Martinetti

Library of Congress Cataloging-in-Publication Data

A catalog record for the print edition is available from the Library of Congress.

Printed in the United States of America

ISBN-10: 0-13-5177928
ISBN-13: 978-0-13-5177921

1   19

CONTENTS

Introduction iv

Acknowledgments vii

From the Author ix

UNIT **1**   Dish Soap for Dinner 2

UNIT **2**   A New Man 6

UNIT **3**   The Runner 10

UNIT **4**   The Love Letters 14

UNIT **5**   Bad Luck, Good Luck 18

UNIT **6**   Lost and Found 22

UNIT **7**   Try, Try Again 26

UNIT **8**   Man's Best Friend 30

UNIT **9**   The Coin 34

UNIT **10** Love or Baseball? 38

UNIT **11** The First Day 42

UNIT **12** The Winning Ticket 46

UNIT **13** Thank You 50

UNIT **14** Together Again 54

UNIT **15** Saved by the Bell 58

UNIT **16** This Is the Place for Me 62

UNIT **17** Nicole's Party 66

UNIT **18** A Strong Little Boy 70

UNIT **19** The Champion 74

UNIT **20** The Bottle 78

UNIT **21** The Last Laugh 82

UNIT **22** Old Friends 86

Key to Guessed Answers 91

Answer Key 93

Credits 104

INTRODUCTION

TRUE STORIES, SILVER EDITION

The Silver Edition of *True Stories* is a five-level reading series. The series is appropriate for beginning to high-intermediate learners of English as a Second or Foreign Language. The Silver Edition consists of revised editions of six of the highly successful and popular *True Stories in the News* books that have provided entertaining stories and effective reading skill instruction for many years. In fact, the first book in that series was published over twenty-five years ago (hence the title "Silver" Edition). The *True Stories* series has been going strong ever since.

NEW IN THE SILVER EDITION

- **New and updated stories.** Some stories have been updated, and some have been replaced with fresh new readings that have been thoroughly classroom-tested before making it into print. All of the readings that have proven to be favorites of students and teachers over the years have been retained.

- **A colorful new design.** Originally published solely in black and white, the new edition has a new full-color design with colorful new photos. The color design makes the readings even more inviting, and the color photos that accompany the readings enhance understanding and enjoyment of the stories.

- **A uniform unit structure.** The books in the series have been given a consistent unit structure that runs across all six books. This predictable structure makes it easy for teachers to teach the series at different levels and for students to progress seamlessly from one level to the next.

- **Audio recordings of every reading.** Every story in the series has been recorded and made available online for students or teachers to download.

- **Online Answer Keys and To the Teacher notes.** In addition to being in the back of the books, as they were in the previous editions, the Answer Keys are now also online as downloadable pdfs. The To the Teacher notes that were previously in the back of the books, however, are now only online. This section provides additional information about the stories and teaching tips. Additional practice activities are also now available online.

THE APPROACH

The underlying premise in this series has always been that when second language learners are engaged in a pleasurable reading experience in the second language, then language learning will take place effortlessly and effectively. The formula is simple: Offer students a true story that fascinates and surprises them. Have them read and enjoy the story. Focus their attention on some useful vocabulary in the story. Confirm that they fully understand the story with reading comprehension exercises. Develop reading skills that progress from basic to more complex. Finally, use the content and the topic of the story to engage in discussion and writing tasks, from tightly structured to more open-ended.

UNIT COMPONENTS

Pre-Reading

Each unit begins with a pre-reading task that piques students' curiosity about the content of the story. Students' attention is drawn to the art that accompanies the reading and the title of the reading as they predict what the story is going to be about.

Reading

The readings are short enough to be read by the students in class; at the lower levels, the stories can be read in minutes. As the levels become higher, the readings do become longer and more challenging. Still, even at the highest levels, each reading and the exercises immediately following it can be completed in one class meeting.

Post-Reading

While there is some variation in the post-reading activities, the following are in all six books:

- **Vocabulary.** Useful key vocabulary items are selected from the readings for presentation and practice. The vocabulary activities vary from unit to unit, and the number of vocabulary items and the extent of the practice increases from level to level.

- **Comprehension.** At least two different comprehension tasks follow the vocabulary section. The exercises have descriptive titles, such as Understanding the Main Ideas, Remembering Details, or Understanding Cause and Effect, so that teachers and students know which cognitive skills are being applied. The exercises have a great deal of variety, keeping students engaged and motivated.

- **Discussion.** Having read and studied the stories, students are encouraged to discuss some aspect arising from the story. Even at the lowest level, students are given simple tasks that will give them the opportunity to talk in pairs, in small groups, or as a whole class.

- **Writing.** The final section of each unit has students produce a short piece of writing related to the reading. Often the writing task derives directly from the Discussion, in which case the title of the section is Discussion/Writing. The writing tasks are level-appropriate and vary in complexity depending on student proficiency. The tasks are not intended to be graded. They simply provide a final opportunity for students to engage with the topic of the reading and deepen their understanding and enjoyment of the story.

TRUE STORIES, LEVEL 2

True Stories, Level 2 is the third book in the Silver Edition of the *True Stories* series. It is intended for high-beginning learners of English. It consists of 22 four-page units, each with the following distinguishing features:

- The pre-reading task has students look at a photo that prompts them to speculate on the content of the story.

- Each story has an average length of 350 words.

- The stories are told in the simple past, past progressive, and future tenses.

- Writing exercises require students to fill in a chart, complete sentences, compose single sentences, or write a short paragraph.

ACKNOWLEDGMENTS

I would like to thank

- the many teachers whose invaluable feedback helped me assess how the stories and exercises were working outside the small sphere of my own classroom. If I were to list you all by name, this acknowledgments section would go on for pages. I would like to thank three colleagues in particular: legendary teacher Peggy Miles, who introduced me to the world of English language teaching; Sharron Bassano, whose innovative techniques for teaching beginning-level students informed my own approach; and Jorge Islas Martinez, whose enthusiasm and dedication remain a constant inspiration;

- my students, who shared personal stories that became the examples for the discussion and writing exercises;

- the people in the stories who supplied details that were not in news sources: Twyla Thompson, John Koehler, Dorothy Peckham, Chi Hsii Tsui, Margaret Patrick, Trish Moore and Rhonda Gill (grandmother and mother of Desiree), Friendship Force participants, Natalie Garibian, Mirsada Buric, and the late Irvin Scott;

- the teachers and editors who made important contributions at different stages of development to the previous editions of these books and whose influence can still be seen throughout this new edition: Allen Ascher, John Barnes, Karen Davy, Joanne Dresner, Nancy Hayward, Stacey Hunter, Penny LaPorte, Laura LeDrean, Françoise Leffler, Linda Moser, Dana Klinek Pinter, Mary Perrotta Rich, Debbie Sistino, and Paula Van Ells;

- Rachel Hayward and Megan Hohenstein, who assisted in piloting and researching new material for the Silver Edition;

- the team at Pearson, whose experienced hands skillfully put together all the moving pieces in the preparation of this Silver Edition: Pietro Alongi, Tracey Cataldo, Warren Fischbach, Lucy Hart, Gosia Jaros-White, Linda Moser, Dana Pinter, Joseph Vella, and Peter West;

- copyeditor and fact checker, Kate Smyres; and proofreader, Ann Dickson;

- editor extraordinaire Françoise Leffler, who lent her expertise to *True Stories* levels 4 and 5;

- Bernard Seal at Page Designs International, who guided this project from start to finish with dedication, creativity, pragmatism, and the occasional "crazy"—but brilliant—idea;

- Don Williams at Page Designs International, whose talent for design is evident on every page; and

- my husband, John Hajdu Heyer, who read the first draft of every story I've considered for the *True Stories* series. The expression on his face as he read told me whether or not the story was a keeper. He didn't know that. Now he does.

FROM THE AUTHOR

Dear Teachers and Students,

This new edition of *True Stories* is the Silver Edition because it celebrates an anniversary— it has been more than 25 years since the first *True Stories* book was published. The way we get our news has changed a lot over the years, but some things have remained the same: Fascinating stories are in the news every day, and the goal of the *True Stories* series is still to bring the best of them to you.

The question students ask most often about these stories is *Are they true?* The answer is *yes*—to the best of my knowledge, these stories are true. I've fact-checked stories by contacting reporters, photojournalists, and research librarians all over the world. I've even called some of the people in the stories to be sure I have the facts right.

Once I'm as sure as I can be that a story is true, the story has to pass one more test. My students read the story, and after they finish reading, they give each story one, two, or three stars. They take this responsibility seriously; they know that only the top-rated stories will become part of the *True Stories* reading series.

I hope that you, too, think these are three-star stories. And I hope that reading them encourages you to share your own stories, which are always the most amazing true stories of all.

Sandra Heyer

UNIT 1

1 PRE-READING

A Look at the picture. Answer the questions.

1. Do you like to eat salad? What is your favorite type of salad?

2. What meal do you like to eat salad with? Lunch? Dinner?

3. What do you like to put on your salad? For example, oil? Lemon juice?

B Read the title of the story. Look at the picture again. Answer the questions.

1. What do you think this story is about?

2. Can you guess what happens?

Dish Soap for Dinner

Joe came home from work and opened his mailbox. In his mailbox, he found a yellow bottle of soap—soap for washing dishes.

The dish soap was a free sample from a soap company. The company mailed small bottles of soap to millions of people. It was a new soap with a little lemon juice in it. The company wanted people to try it.

Joe looked at his free bottle of soap. There was a picture of two lemons on the label. Over the lemons were the words "with Real Lemon Juice."

"Good!" Joe thought. "A free sample of lemon juice! I'm going to have a salad for dinner. This lemon juice will taste good on my salad." Joe put the soap on his salad and ate it. After Joe ate the salad, he felt sick.

Joe wasn't the only person who got sick. A lot of people thought the soap was lemon juice. They put the soap on fish, on salads, and in tea. Later they felt sick, too. Some people had stomachaches, but felt better in a few hours. Some people felt really sick and went to the hospital. Luckily, no one died from eating the soap.

What can we learn from Joe's story? Read labels carefully. And don't eat dish soap for dinner!

2 VOCABULARY

Complete the sentences. Find the right words. Circle the letter of the answer.

1. The dish soap was a _____ from a soap company.
   a. letter
   b. free sample
   c. mailbox

2. The company wanted people to _____ the soap.
   a. try
   b. eat
   c. mail

3. There was a picture of two lemons on the _____.
   a. soap company
   b. label
   c. salad

4. Joe thought, "This lemon juice will _____ good on my salad."
   a. look
   b. taste
   c. feel

5. What can we learn from Joe's story? Read labels _____.
   a. fast
   b. happily
   c. carefully

3 COMPREHENSION

REMEMBERING DETAILS

One word in each sentence is not correct. Find the word and cross it out. Write the correct word.

1. In his mailbox, Joe found a ~~green~~ *yellow* bottle of soap.

2. The dish soap was a free ticket from a soap company.

3. It was a new soap with a little orange juice in it.

4. The company wanted people to eat it.

5. There was a picture of two bananas on the label.

6. Joe put the soap on his dishes.

7. After he ate the salad, Joe felt fine.

8. A lot of people thought the soup was lemon juice.

9. They put the soap on fish, on salads, and in coffee.

UNDERSTANDING CAUSE AND EFFECT

Find the best way to complete each sentence. Write the letter of the answer on the line.

1. The company mailed soap to people __d__

2. There was a picture of two lemons on the label _____

3. Joe put the soap on his salad _____

4. Some people went to the hospital _____

a. because they ate the soap and got sick.

b. because he thought the soap was lemon juice.

c. because the soap had a little lemon juice in it.

d. because it wanted people to try the soap.

UNDERSTANDING A SUMMARY

Imagine this: You want to tell the story "Dish Soap for Dinner" to a friend. You want to tell the story quickly, in only two sentences. Which two sentences tell the story best? Check (✓) your answer.

☐ 1. Joe came home from work and opened his mailbox. He was happy because he found a free sample—a yellow bottle of dish soap.

☑ 2. A soap company mailed soap to millions of people. Some people thought the soap was lemon juice, so they ate it and got sick.

4 DISCUSSION

Joe made a mistake: He thought the dish soap was lemon juice. People make mistakes when they don't read labels carefully. They often make mistakes in other situations, too—when they travel, shop, cook, or use technology.

A Do you have a story about a mistake you made? On the lines below, write a few sentences about your experience. Here, for example, is what one student wrote.

I made a mistake when I traveled by subway. I wanted to go to the library, but I went to a town called Library.

_____

_____

_____

B Share your experience in a small group. Try not to read your sentences. Look at your classmates as you tell your story.

5 WRITING

A Read Joe's story again. It's in the present tense.

Joe comes home from work and opens his mailbox. In his mailbox, he finds a free sample of dish soap. The dish soap has a little lemon juice in it.

Joe looks at his bottle of soap. There is a picture of two lemons on the label. Over the lemons are the words "with Real Lemon Juice."

Joe thinks the soap is lemon juice. He puts it on his salad and eats it. After he eats the salad, he feels sick. Poor Joe!

B On the lines below, write the story again in the past tense. The first sentence is done for you.

Joe came home from work and opened his mailbox.

_____

_____

_____

_____

_____

_____

UNIT 2

1 PRE-READING

A Look at the picture. Answer the questions.

1. Whose pants is the man wearing?

2. Why is he excited?

3. What changes can people make in their lives to be healthier? Do you sometimes make changes to be healthier?

B Read the title of the story. Think about the picture again. Answer the questions.

1. What do you think this story is about?

2. Can you guess what happens?

A New Man

Roley McIntyre was a big man—he was a very big man. He weighed 600 pounds (272 kilograms).

For lunch Roley ate ten pieces of bacon, four eggs, ten potatoes, and fried vegetables. For dinner he ate meat and more potatoes, and after dinner he always ate dessert. Before he went to bed, he ate a few sandwiches and some cake.

Roley couldn't drive a regular car because he was too big. He couldn't fit in the front seat. Roley had a special car. It had no front seat. Roley drove his car from the back seat.

One day Roley went to the doctor. The doctor said, "Mr. McIntyre, you have a special car. Now you need to buy a special coffin—a coffin for a very big man. You have to lose weight, or you're going to die soon."

Roley went on a diet. For breakfast he ate cereal with nonfat milk. For lunch he ate baked beans on toast. For dinner he ate fish and vegetables.

After Roley began to lose weight, he met a woman named Josephine. She told Roley, "Don't stop your diet."

Roley didn't stop his diet. He continued to lose weight. In 18 months, he lost 400 pounds (181 kilograms). Then six months after that, he and Josephine got married.

After they got married, Roley bought a new car. His old car was special—it had no front seat. His new car had three rows—a front seat and two back seats. Roley bought a big car not because he was a big man. He bought it because he and Josephine wanted a big family. It was a big car for a big family. It was a new car for a new man.

2 VOCABULARY

Complete the sentences. Find the right words. Circle the letter of the answer.

1. After dinner Roley ate cake, cookies, or ice cream. He always ate _____.
   a. lunch
   b. dessert
   c. breakfast

2. Roley couldn't drive a regular car because he was too big. He couldn't _____ in the front seat.
   a. fit
   b. stand
   c. see

3. The doctor told Roley, "You have a special car. Now you need to buy a special _____ because you're going to die soon."
   a. refrigerator
   b. garage
   c. coffin

4. The doctor told Roley, "You are too big. You have to go on a diet. Don't eat potatoes and dessert. You need to _____."
   a. eat more
   b. lose weight
   c. buy clothes

3 COMPREHENSION

LOOKING FOR DETAILS

A What did Roley eat when he was big? Find the words in the story. Write them on the lines below.

<u>bacon</u>   potatoes   _____

<u>eggs</u>   fried vegetables   _____

meat   dessert   _____

sandwiches   milkshake   _____

B What did Roley eat when he was on a diet? Find the words in the story. Write them on the lines below.

<u>cereal with nonfat milk</u>   _____

baked beans on toast   vegetables   _____

REVIEWING THE STORY

Complete each sentence. Then read the story again and check your answers.

Roley McIntyre was very big. He _____<u>weighed</u>_____ 600 pounds. Roley couldn't drive a

                                                        1.

regular car. He couldn't fit in the front _____, so Roley's car had no front seat. He

                                                              2.

could drive his car from the _____ seat.

                                           3.

Roley's doctor said, "Mr. McIntyre, you have to lose weight, or you're going to _____

                                                                         4.

soon." Roley went on a _____. He began to lose _____. He met

                                        5.   6.

a _____. Her name was Josephine. She told Roley, "Don't

                  7.

_____ your diet." Roley didn't stop his diet; he lost 400 _____.

                  8.   9.

Two years after Roley started his diet, Roley and Josephine got _____.

                                                                   10.

UNDERSTANDING CAUSE AND EFFECT

Find the best way to complete each sentence. Write the letter of the answer on the line.

1. Roley McIntyre was big <u>c</u>

2. Roley couldn't drive a regular car _____

3. Roley needed to buy a coffin _____

4. Roley ate only fish and vegetables for dinner _____

5. Roley bought a big new car with three rows of seats _____

a. because he was going to die.

b. because he was on a diet.

c. because he ate a lot.

d. because he couldn't fit in the front seat.

e. because he and Josephine wanted to have a big family

4 WRITING / DISCUSSION

A What did you usually eat for breakfast, lunch, dinner, and snacks in your native country? What do you usually eat in the United States? Complete the chart.

	IN MY NATIVE COUNTRY, I USUALLY ATE...	IN THE UNITED STATES, I USUALLY EAT...
Breakfast		
Lunch		
Dinner		
Snacks		

B Take turns reading your chart to a partner.

C Answer the questions below. Write complete sentences.

1. Do you and your partner eat the same food?

_____

_____

_____

2. Which food do you think is healthier—the food you ate in your native country or the food you eat in the United States?

_____

_____

_____

UNIT 3

1 PRE-READING

A Look at the picture. Answer the questions.

1. Why do people run? Do you like to run?

2. Is it unusual to see older people running in the street?

B Read the title of the story. Think about the picture again. Answer the questions.

1. What do you think this story is about?

2. Can you guess what happens?

The Runner

One morning a man was driving to work when he saw something unusual: An old woman was running along the street. The man called the police on his cell phone. "I saw a very old woman on Torggate Street," he said. "She was running. Maybe she escaped from a nursing home. Please try to find her."

Two police officers drove to Torggate Street. An old woman was running along the street. The man was right: She was very old—maybe 80 or 90. The police officers stopped their car and ran after the woman.

"Ma'am, please stop!" they said.

The old woman stopped and turned around.

"Are you OK?" the police officers asked.

"Yes, I'm fine," the woman said.

"What's your name, please?" the police officers asked.

"Sigrid Krohn," the woman answered.

"Mrs. Krohn, do you live near here?"

"About a kilometer away," she answered. Mrs. Krohn gave the officers her address.

One of the police officers wrote down the address, walked back to his car, and called the police station. A few minutes later, he returned.

"It's all correct," he told the other police officer. "She lives in her own home, about a kilometer from here."

"Of course it's correct," Mrs. Krohn said. "There's nothing wrong with my head." Then she patted her legs and smiled. "And there's nothing wrong with my legs."

"Do you mind telling us how old you are?" the police officers asked.

"No, I don't mind," the woman said. "I'm 94."

"You're 94?" the police officers asked.

"That's correct," Mrs. Krohn answered.

"One more question," the police officers said. "Do you mind telling us why you're running?"

Mrs. Krohn looked surprised. "I'm running for exercise," she answered. "Twice a week, I run a kilometer or two. Is it OK if I continue?"

"Of course. Go ahead," the police officers said. "We're sorry we bothered you."

"No problem," Mrs. Krohn said, and she ran away on her old, strong legs.

2 VOCABULARY

Which words have the same meaning as the words in *italics*? Write the letter of the answer on the line.

_b_ 1. The man thought, "Maybe the old woman *escaped* from a nursing home."

____ 2. Mrs. Krohn's house was only a kilometer away. It was *near* Torggate Street.

____ 3. The police officer *returned* to his car.

____ 4. Mrs. Krohn *patted* her legs several times with her hands.

____ 5. The police officers asked Mrs. Krohn, "Do you mind telling us how old you are?" She answered, "No, *I don't mind*."

a. touched

b. ran away

c. went back

d. It's OK with me.

e. not far from

3 PRACTICING PRONUNCIATION

The underlined words are in the story. If you can say them correctly, you can say the words below them correctly, too. Practice with your teacher.

call	old	man	right	pat
ball	cold	can	fight	cat
fall	hold	pan	light	hat
hall	sold	ran	night	rat
tall	told	van	tight	sat

4 COMPREHENSION

REMEMBERING DETAILS

Complete the sentences. Write the answers on the lines.

1. The old woman was walking, right?

   No, she wasn't. She was _running_____.

2. The man thought, "Maybe she escaped from a prison," right?

   No, he didn't. He thought, "Maybe she escaped from a _____."

3. Two paramedics drove to Torggate Street, right?

   No, two _____.

4. The woman lived about three kilometers away, right?

   No, she didn't. She lived about _____.

5. She gave the police officers her telephone number, right?

   No, she didn't. She gave them her _____.

6. The police officer called the police station and returned in a few hours, right?

   No, he didn't. He returned in a few _____.

7. She was 84 years old, right?

   No, she wasn't. She was _____.

8. The woman runs three times a week, right?

   No, she doesn't. She runs _____.

UNDERSTANDING DIALOGUE

A Match the questions and the answers. Write the letter of the answer on the line.

_c_ 1. "Are you OK?"

_____ 2. "What's your name, please?"

_____ 3. "Do you live near here?"

_____ 4. "How old are you?"

_____ 5. "Why are you running?"

a. "I'm 94."

b. "Yes, about a kilometer away."

c. "Yes, I'm fine."

d. "I'm running for exercise."

e. "Mrs. Krohn."

B The five questions and answers above make a short conversation. Practice the conversation with a partner. One student reads the questions; the other student reads the answers.

5 WRITING/DISCUSSION

A Think about an old person you know and like. Complete the sentences.

1. I am thinking about _____.

2. He/She is _____ years old.

3. He/She lives in _____.

4. Every day he/she _____

_____

_____.

5. When he/she was young, he/she _____

_____

_____.

6. I like him/her because _____

_____

_____.

B Read the sentences you wrote above to a partner. Tell your partner a little more about the person.

UNIT 4

1 PRE-READING

A Look at the picture. Answer the questions.

1. Do you like to receive letters in the mail? What kinds of letters do you like to receive?

2. How often do you write a letter? When do you write letters?

B Read the title of the story. Look at the picture again. Answer the questions.

1. What do you think this story is about?

2. Can you guess what happens?

The Love Letters

Ming-fu and Lee met at a party. For Ming-fu, it was love at first sight. "Hello," he said to Lee. "I'm Ming-fu." Lee looked at him and smiled. "Hi," she said. "I'm Lee." Ming-fu and Lee laughed and talked all evening. When they left the party, it was 2 a.m.

For the next year, Ming-fu and Lee were together every weekend. They went everywhere together—to movies, to parks, to museums, and to restaurants.

One night at a romantic restaurant, Ming-fu asked Lee, "Will you marry me?" "No," Lee answered. "I'm not ready to get married."

"I can't believe it!" Ming-fu thought. "Lee doesn't want to marry me! But I love her! What can I do?" Ming-fu began writing love letters to Lee. Every day he wrote a letter and mailed it to her. "I love you," he said in his letters. "Marry me."

Every day the same mail carrier delivered Ming-fu's letter to Lee. The mail carrier always smiled when he gave Lee a letter. "Another letter from your boyfriend," he said.

Ming-fu sent Lee a love letter every day for two years—700 letters altogether. Finally Lee said, "I'm ready to get married now."

Did Lee marry Ming-fu? No, she didn't. She married the mail carrier who delivered Ming-fu's letters.

2 VOCABULARY

Complete the sentences with the words below.

altogether	can't believe it	delivered	love at first sight	ready

1. When Ming-fu met Lee, he loved her immediately. It was _love at first sight_ .

2. Lee told Ming-fu, "I don't want to get married now. It's not a good time for me. I'm not _____ to get married now."

3. When Lee told Ming-fu, "I'm not ready to get married," Ming-fu was very surprised. "This is not possible!" he thought. "I _____ !"

4. Every day the same mail carrier took Ming-fu's letter to Lee's house. Then he gave the letter to Lee. He _____ Ming-fu's letter.

5. Ming-fu wrote six or seven letters every week for two years—700 letters _____ .

3 COMPREHENSION

UNDERSTANDING WORD GROUPS

Read each group of words. One word in each group doesn't belong. Find the word and cross it out.

smile	parks	marry	mail carrier
~~run~~	museums	romantic	~~doctor~~
laugh	~~labels~~	love	letters
talk	restaurants	~~soccer~~	send

REMEMBERING DETAILS

One word in each sentence is not correct. Find the word and cross it out. Write the correct word.

1. Ming-fu and Lee met at a ~~concert~~. *party*

2. When they left the party, it was 2 p.m.

3. For the next year, Ming-fu and Lee were together every morning.

4. They went everywhere together—to movies, to parks, to museums, and to schools.

5. One night, at a romantic restaurant, Ming-fu asked Lee, "Will you write me?"

6. Ming-fu began writing postcards to Lee.

7. Ming-fu sent Lee a love letter every day—70 letters altogether.

8. Lee married the mail carrier who wrote Ming-fu's letters.

UNDERSTANDING QUOTATIONS

Find the best way to complete each sentence. Write the letter of the answer on the line.

1. When Ming-fu met Lee, he said, __c__

2. When Ming-fu asked Lee, "Will you marry me?" she said, _____

3. When Ming-fu wrote love letters to Lee, he told her, _____

4. When the mail carrier delivered Ming-fu's letters, he smiled and said, _____

a. "Another letter from your boyfriend."

b. "I love you. Marry me."

c. "Hello. I'm Ming-fu."

d. "No. I'm not ready to get married."

4 DISCUSSION

When Lee told Ming-fu, "I'm not ready to get married," Ming-fu thought, "What can I do?"

A What can Ming-fu do? Read the list below with the help of your dictionary or your teacher. Choose the five best ideas. Check (✓) them.

Ming-fu wants Lee to marry him. What can he do? He can...

☐ 1. write love letters to her.

☐ 2. call her on the phone every day.

☐ 3. sing to her.

☐ 4. buy her presents (flowers, candy, jewelry).

☐ 5. take her to restaurants for dinner.

☐ 6. cook for her.

☐ 7. take her dancing.

☐ 8. wear nice clothes.

☐ 9. be clean and smell good.

☐ 10. listen to her when she talks.

☐ 11. always tell her the truth. Never lie to her.

☐ 12. remember important days—her birthday, for example.

☐ 13. be polite; say "please" and "thank you."

☐ 14. tell her she is beautiful.

☐ 15. be faithful to her. (No other girlfriends!)

B Tell a partner the five best ideas. Explain why you think the ideas will help Ming-fu win Lee. Your partner can agree or disagree.

C Do you have an idea that is not on the list above? Share it with the class.

5 WRITING

A What do people write in a love letter? Make a list of possible sentences with your classmates. Your teacher will write your sentences on the board.

B Ming-fu and Lee lived in Taiwan, so Ming-fu wrote his letters in Chinese. On your own paper, write a love letter from Ming-fu to Lee in English. (You can use the sentences on the board.)

UNIT 5

1 PRE-READING

A Look at the picture on the left. Answer the questions.

1. What is the problem with the car?

2. How do you think it happened?

B Look at the picture on the right. Answer the questions.

1. Do you sometimes order food for delivery to your door? What do you order? How do you pay for the food?

2. Why is this man going to someone's door?

C Read the title of the story. Look at the pictures again. Answer the questions.

1. What do you think this story is about?

2. Can you guess what happens?

Bad Luck, Good Luck

Vegard Olsen is 24 years old. He lives alone, but he visits his parents often. On a Saturday evening, Vegard went to his parents' house for dinner. After dinner, he went to his car to drive home. "Oh, no!" he thought when he saw his car. "My car window is broken! Maybe someone broke into my car!"

Vegard got in the car and looked under the front seat. He usually kept his wallet there. His wallet was gone. In his wallet there was some cash, his driver's license, and his credit card. Vegard called the police. Then he called his credit card company. "My credit card was stolen," he told the company.

Vegard got into his car to drive home. He usually listened to music when he drove. That evening he didn't want to listen to music. It was a quiet ride home.

Vegard works at a pizza restaurant. On Monday he delivered a pizza and some soft drinks to a house near the restaurant. A young man answered the door.

"How much is it?" the man asked Vegard.

"$22.89," Vegard answered.

"Can I pay with a credit card?" the man asked.

"Sure," Vegard said.

The man gave Vegard a credit card. It was Vegard's card! Vegard wanted to say, "Hey! This is my card! Give me my wallet!" But he didn't. He said, "Enjoy your pizza. Have a nice evening." Then he went back to the restaurant and called the police.

The police went to the man's house. Inside they found Vegard's wallet. The cash was gone, but his driver's license and credit card were in the wallet. The police gave everything back to Vegard.

That night Vegard drove home from work with his wallet in his pocket. He listened to music, and he sang along with every song. He smiled all the way home.

2 VOCABULARY

Complete the sentences with the words below.

| broke into | cash | delivered | stolen | wallet |

1. Vegard's money, driver's license, and credit card were in his _____ *wallet* _____.

2. Someone broke a car window and took things from Vegard's car. Vegard called the police and said, "Someone _____ my car."

3. Someone took Vegard's credit card. Vegard called the credit card company and said, "My card was _____."

4. A man ordered pizza and soft drinks. Vegard drove to the man's house and _____ the food.

5. Vegard got his credit card back, but not his money. The _____ was gone.

3 PRACTICING PRONUNCIATION

The underlined words are in the story. If you can say them correctly, you can say the words below them correctly, too. Practice with your teacher.

car	cash	back	found	nice	can
bar	cab	black	ground	mice	Dan
far	cap	crack	pound	price	fan
jar	cat	pack	round	rice	man
star	catch	sack	sound	twice	tan

4 COMPREHENSION

UNDERSTANDING THE MAIN IDEAS

Circle the letter of the correct answer.

1. When Vegard saw the broken car window, he said, "Oh, no!" because
   a. it is expensive to fix a broken window.
   b. he thought, "Maybe someone broke into my car."

2. Vegard looked under the seat because
   a. he usually kept his wallet there.
   b. he usually kept his car keys there.

3. He called his credit card company because
   a. he wanted more credit.
   b. his card was stolen.

4. It was a quiet ride home because
   a. there were no cars on the streets.
   b. Vegard didn't want to listen to music.

5. Two days later, Vegard smiled all the way home because
   a. he had his wallet back.
   b. he liked to work at the pizza restaurant.

REMEMBERING DETAILS

Read the summary of the story "Bad Luck, Good Luck." There are eight mistakes in the summary. Find the mistakes and cross them out. Write the correct words. The first one is done for you.

Vegard Olsen visited his parents on a Saturday ~~morning~~ *evening*. Then he went to his truck to

drive home. A car window was dirty. "Maybe someone broke into my car!" he thought.

Vegard got in the car and looked under the back seat. His purse was gone.

Vegard works at a hamburger restaurant. On Wednesday, he delivered a pizza to a house near the restaurant. A woman paid for the pizza with Vegard's credit card. Vegard called the police.

The police went to the house. They found Vegard's things and gave them back to him.

5 DISCUSSION

A Someone broke into Vegard's car and took his wallet. That was a crime. Read the list of crimes below. Check (✓) the crimes that sometimes happen in your native city.

- ☐ break into a car
- ☐ take a wallet or purse
- ☐ hit someone and then take his or her money
- ☐ go into someone's house and take things
- ☐ take things from a store
- ☐ go into a store or bank and take money
- ☐ take a car
- ☐ drive while drunk
- ☐ write with paint on buildings
- ☐ sell drugs
- ☐ kill someone
- ☐ _____

(other)

B Read the crimes you checked to a partner who comes from a different city from you. Then answer the questions below.

1. Did you and your partner check the same crimes?
2. What is the punishment for those crimes in your native country?
3. Do you have any experience with crime? For example, did someone take your wallet? Tell your partner about it.
4. What can you do so crimes don't happen to you?

6 WRITING

A Write a sentence about the story. The sentence can be true, or it can be false. For example:

Vegard Olsen works at a pizza restaurant. (true)
He lives with his parents. (false)

B Copy your sentence on the board. Your classmates will read the sentence and say if it is true or false.

Bob, Eddy, and David

1 PRE-READING

A Look at the picture. Answer the questions.

1. What is the relationship between the three boys in the picture—Bob, Eddy, and David?

2. Why do you think they look so happy?

B Read the title of the story. Look at the picture again. Answer the questions.

1. What do you think this story is about?

2. Can you guess what happens?

Lost and Found

Bob Shafran was happy. He was at a new school, and the other students were friendly. "Hi, Bob!" they said. But some students said, "Hi, Eddy!" Bob didn't understand. He asked another student, "Why do some students call me Eddy?"

"Oh, that's easy to explain," the student said. "Eddy Galland was a student here last year. Now he goes to a different school. You look like Eddy. Some students think that you're Eddy."

Bob wanted to meet Eddy Galland. He got Eddy's address from a student and went to Eddy's house. Eddy opened the door. Bob couldn't believe his eyes. He and Eddy looked exactly alike! They had the same color eyes and the same smile. They had the same dark, curly hair. They also had the same birthday. And they both were adopted.

Bob and Eddy found out that they were twin brothers. Soon after the boys were born, one family adopted Bob, and another family adopted Eddy. Bob's family never knew about Eddy, and Eddy's family never knew about Bob.

Bob and Eddy's story was in the newspaper. There was a photo of Bob and Eddy next to the story. A young man named David Kellman saw the photo in the newspaper. David couldn't believe his eyes. He looked exactly like Bob and Eddy! He had the same color eyes and the same smile. He had the same dark, curly hair. He had the same birthday. And he, too, was adopted.

Later, David met Bob and Eddy. When Bob and Eddy saw David, they couldn't believe their eyes. David looked exactly like them! Why did David look exactly like Bob and Eddy? You can probably guess. Bob and Eddy were not twins. Bob, Eddy, and David were triplets.

2 VOCABULARY

Complete the sentences with the words below.

adopted	call	exactly	found out	guessed

1. Some students said, "Hi, Eddy!" Bob told another student, "That's not my name. Why do some students _____*call*_____ me Eddy?"

2. Soon after Bob was born, the Shafran family _____ him. He had a new mother and father and a new family.

3. Bob didn't know about Eddy, and Eddy didn't know about Bob. But later they learned that they were brothers. They _____ that they were twin brothers.

4. Bob, Eddy, and David had the same eyes, the same smile, and the same hair. Everything was the same. David looked _____ like Bob and Eddy.

5. When David saw the newspaper photo of Bob and Eddy, he wasn't sure they were his brothers. But he _____ they probably were.

3 COMPREHENSION

UNDERSTANDING THE MAIN IDEAS

Circle the letter of the best answer.

1. What was "lost and found"?
   a. students
   b. brothers
   c. parents

2. How did Bob meet Eddy?
   a. He got Eddy's address and went to his house.
   b. He sat next to Eddy at school.
   c. He went to Eddy's birthday party.

3. Bob, Eddy, and David were brothers. They didn't know that. Why?
   a. They didn't have the same last name.
   b. They didn't look alike: They had different smiles and noses.
   c. Their parents didn't tell them because they didn't know.

LOOKING FOR DETAILS

Find four correct ways to complete the sentence. Check (✓) your answers.

Bob, Eddy, and David had the same...

☐ color eyes.	☐ dark, curly hair.
☐ smile.	☐ birthday.
☐ last name.	☐ address.

UNDERSTANDING CAUSE AND EFFECT

Find the best way to complete each sentence. Write the letter of the answer on the line.

1. Bob Shafran was happy at his new school _e_

2. Bob never saw Eddy at school _____

3. Some students called Bob "Eddy" _____

4. Bob Shafran didn't know he had a brother _____

5. David looked exactly like Bob and Eddy _____

a. because Eddy went to a different school.

b. because Bob looked like Eddy Galland.

c. because his family never knew about Eddy.

d. because Bob, Eddy, and David were triplets.

e. because the other students were friendly.

4 DISCUSSION / WRITING

David looked like Bob and Eddy. What about your family? Are there people who look alike?

A Think about two people in your family who look alike—for example, you and your mother; your two brothers; your cousin and your grandfather. Write their names on the lines below.

_____ and _____

B How are the two people the same? Check (✓) the words that describe them.

Both have the same...	*Both have...*	*Both are...*
☐ color eyes.	☐ curly hair.	☐ tall.
☐ color hair.	☐ straight hair.	☐ short.
☐ color skin.	☐ big eyes.	☐ average height.
☐ smile.	☐ big feet.	☐ thin.
☐ teeth.	☐ small feet.	☐ a little heavy.
☐ nose.	☐ big hands.	☐ average weight.
☐ eyebrows.	☐ glasses.	☐ strong.

C Read the words you checked to a partner. Tell your partner a little more about the people in your family who look alike.

D Use the information above to write a paragraph. For example, you can begin:

Lina and I are sisters. We have the same color eyes and hair.

_____

_____

_____

_____

_____

_____

_____

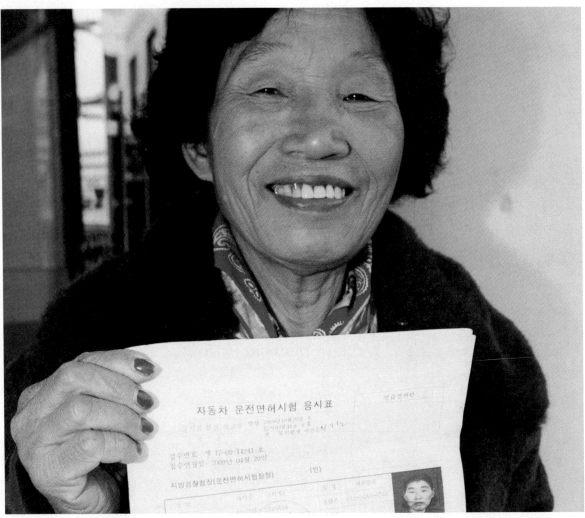

Mrs. Sa Soon Cha

1 PRE-READING

A Look at the picture. Answer the questions.

1. The woman in the picture—Sa Soon Cha—looks very happy. Why do you think she is happy?

2. Mrs. Cha is holding a piece of paper. What do you think the paper is about?

B Read the title of the story. Look at the picture again. Answer the questions.

1. What do you think this story is about?

2. Can you guess what happens?

Try, Try Again

Sa Soon Cha was a 69-year-old widow. She lived alone in a small house in South Korea. Behind her house, Mrs. Cha had a vegetable garden.

Every morning she got up early and picked vegetables in her garden. Then she packed up the vegetables, got on a bus, and took the vegetables to a market. She sold the vegetables at the market.

It was a long bus ride to the market—about an hour. And it was difficult to carry the vegetables on and off the bus. Why did Mrs. Cha take the bus? She didn't have a car. Why didn't she have a car? She didn't have a driver's license.

Mrs. Cha wanted to get her license. Then she could buy a car and drive to the market. She studied for the driver's license test. Then she took the test. It was a difficult test, with 40 questions. Mrs. Cha didn't pass it.

Mrs. Cha had only a little education, and reading was difficult for her. The test had some long words, like *emergency*. They were not easy to read. Mrs. Cha studied more and took the test again. She didn't pass it.

Mrs. Cha made a sign and put it on a wall in her house. "Never give up!" the sign said. Mrs. Cha didn't give up. During the next four years, she took the test 950 times. Finally, she passed it. Next, she had to take a road test. That test was easier for Mrs. Cha. She passed it on her fifth try.

Mrs. Cha's story was in the news. People at a Korean car company read about Mrs. Cha, and they sent her a letter. "Congratulations!" the letter said. But the company gave Mrs. Cha more than a letter. They gave her a car!

Now Mrs. Cha drives to the market in her beautiful new car.

2 VOCABULARY

Complete the sentences with the words below.

about	give up	packed up	pass	widow

1. Sa Soon Cha has no husband. He died a few years ago. She is a _____widow_____ .

2. Mrs. Cha _____ the vegetables for the bus ride. She put them in bags.

3. Mrs. Cha's bus ride was usually 60 minutes. Sometimes it was a little shorter, and sometimes it was a little longer. It was _____ an hour.

4. The test had 40 questions. Mrs. Cha had only 16 correct answers. She didn't _____ the test.

5. Mrs. Cha didn't stop studying for the test. She took the test many times and finally passed it. She didn't _____ .

3 COMPREHENSION

REMEMBERING DETAILS

Circle the correct word or phrase.

1. Mrs. Cha took the (bus / train) to the market.

2. She wanted to buy a (car / truck).

3. The driver's license test was (easy / difficult) for her.

4. The test had some long words, like (emergency / vegetables).

5. (Reading / Speaking) was difficult for Mrs. Cha.

6. She took the test (95 / 950) times.

7. Finally, she (passed the test / gave up).

8. A Korean company gave her a new (car / house).

9. Now Mrs. Cha (walks / drives) to the market.

ORGANIZING INFORMATION

Look at the list of things that Mrs. Cha did every day before she passed the driver's license test and got a car. Then write two lists: what she does now and what she doesn't do now.

She got up early.	She got on a bus.
She studied for the test.	She rode the bus to the market.
She picked vegetables.	She sold vegetables.

WHAT SHE DOES NOW	WHAT SHE DOESN'T DO NOW
She gets up early.	She doesn't study for the test.

FINDING MORE INFORMATION

Read each sentence on the left. Which sentence on the right gives you more information? Write the letter of the answer on the line. (The information on the right is not in the story, but it is true.)

_b_ 1. Mrs. Cha's house was small.

_____ 2. She lived in South Korea.

_____ 3. She got up early.

_____ 4. She took the bus to the market.

_____ 5. She had only a little education.

_____ 6. She took the test 950 times.

_____ 7. A Korean car company gave her a new car.

a. Its value was $17,000.

b. It had only one room.

c. She went to school only a few years.

d. She woke up at 4 a.m.

e. When she passed it, her driving teachers hugged her.

f. It came by her house every two hours.

g. Her village was 112 miles south of Seoul.

4 WRITING / DISCUSSION

Mrs. Cha made a sign and put it on a wall in her house. "Never give up!" the sign said. The sign helped her pass her driving test and get her driver's license.

A Think of a sign in your native language that can help you. Write the sign below in English. Here are examples of what some students wrote.

If a big rock is in your way, don't push it. Go around it.

What I want to do, I can do.

Next September, I'm going to be in English class Level 3.

B Show your sign to your classmates. Tell them the meaning of your sign. Explain how the sign helps you.

UNIT 8

1 PRE-READING

A Look at the picture. Answer the questions.

1. Where is this house?

2. How old is it?

3. Can you guess who lived there?

B Read the title of the story. Look at the picture again. Answer the questions.

1. What do you think this story is about?

2. Can you guess what happens?

Man's Best Friend

A long time ago, in a small house in Scotland, two friends lived together. Their names were John and Bobby.

John and Bobby were not rich, but they were happy. They had a warm fire when it was cold outside. They had good food to eat when they were hungry. They were never lonely because they had each other.

John and Bobby liked to take long walks together. After their walk, John usually cooked dinner. John and Bobby ate dinner and then sat in front of the fire. They had a simple but good life.

Then, in the spring of 1858, John got sick and died. He was buried in a cemetery in Edinburgh, Scotland. After John was buried, Bobby stood at John's grave and cried. "Come on, Bobby," friends said. "It's time to go home." Bobby went home, but later he returned to the cemetery. He sat down near John's grave. He stayed there all night.

Bobby stayed at the cemetery the next day, and the next day, and the next. For the next 14 years, Bobby never left the cemetery. When the weather was cold or rainy, he slept in a small house at the cemetery. When the weather was warm, he slept on the ground near John's grave.

Finally, in 1872, Bobby died, too. Friends buried him in a little grave near John. Why was Bobby's grave little? Bobby, John's best friend, was a dog.

2 VOCABULARY

Complete the sentences with the words below.

a long time ago	grave	ground	lonely	simple

1. This story is from the 1800s. That was _a long time ago_.

2. John had no wife or children, but he had his dog, Bobby. John and Bobby were always together. So, John was not alone, and he was not sad. He was not _____.

3. Every day John took a long walk with his dog. Then he went home to his small house and cooked dinner. After dinner he sat in front of the fire. John had a _____ life.

4. John was buried in a cemetery in Edinburgh. After he was buried, Bobby stood at John's _____ and cried.

5. When the weather was cold or rainy, Bobby slept in a small house at the cemetery. But when the weather was warm, he slept outside, on the _____.

3 COMPREHENSION

REMEMBERING DETAILS

One word in each sentence is not correct. Find the word and cross it out. Write the correct word.

small

1. Two friends lived together in a ~~big~~ house in Scotland.

2. Their names were John and Sammy.

3. In the spring of 1958, John got sick and died.

4. He was buried in a cemetery in Edinburgh, Ireland.

5. Bobby lived in the cemetery for four years.

6. When Bobby died, friends buried him in a large grave.

7. Bobby, John's best friend, was a man.

REVIEWING THE STORY

Complete each sentence. Then read the story again and check your answers.

John and Bobby lived together in a small house. They were not _____*rich*_____,

1.

but they were happy. They had a warm _____ when it was cold outside.

2.

They had good food to eat when they were _____. They were never

3.

_____ because they had each other.

4.

After John died, Bobby lived in the cemetery. When the weather was cold or

_____, he slept in a small house at the cemetery. When the

5.

_____ was warm, he slept on the ground near John's grave. He lived in the

6.

cemetery for 14 _____, until he died in 1872.

7.

FINDING CLUES IN THE STORY

When did you know that Bobby was a dog—at the end of the story or before the end? Which sentences in the story tell you that maybe Bobby was a dog? Underline them. Then read the sentences to the class.

4 WRITING / DISCUSSION

After Bobby died, the people of Edinburgh put a statue of Bobby outside the cemetery. Every year thousands of tourists go to Edinburgh to see Bobby's grave and his statue.

The Statue of Bobby

A Think about a city you know very well. Is there a place tourists always visit—a building, a park, a bridge, or a statue? Draw a picture of it in the space below.

B Write about the place in your picture. Complete the sentences.

The name of this place is _____ .

It is in _____ .

Many people go there because _____

_____

I think it is _____ .

C Read your sentences to a partner. Show your partner your drawing. Tell your partner a little more about the place you drew.

UNIT 9

1 PRE-READING

A Look at the picture. Answer the questions.

1. On what special occasions do people make cakes?

2. Do people sometimes put objects inside special cakes? Why?

B Read the title of the story. Look at the picture again. Answer the questions.

1. What do you think this story is about?

2. Can you guess what happens?

The Coin

It was December 25. Marie Orr, a 13-year-old Australian girl, was happy. It was Christmas, and Marie's mother was making a special cake for dessert. Her mother put four small coins into the cake; then she baked it. The four coins were for good luck.

After dinner Marie and her family ate the cake. They found three coins in the cake and put them on the table. Where was the fourth coin? It was missing, but Marie's mother didn't notice.

After Christmas Marie got sick. She coughed, and she couldn't speak. After six weeks, she felt better, but she still couldn't speak. Marie's parents took her to the hospital.

Doctors at the hospital looked at Marie. They took an X-ray of her throat. Marie's parents asked the doctors, "Why can't Marie speak?" The doctors said, "We don't know. Maybe she will speak again. Maybe she won't. We're sorry, but we can't help her."

For 12 years, Marie didn't speak. She grew up, she got a job, and she got married. But she never spoke.

One day when Marie was 25 years old, she got a sore throat at work. She began to cough. She coughed up something small and black. What was it? Marie didn't know. She took it to the hospital. A doctor at the hospital said, "This is a coin!"

The doctor told Marie, "I think you can speak again." Marie went to a special doctor, and soon she was talking.

What a story Marie can tell!

2 VOCABULARY

Complete the sentences with the words below.

coins	coughed	missing	notice	throat

1. At Christmas many Australians put money in their cakes. Marie's mother put four small _____*coins*_____ in her cake.

2. There were only three coins on the table. Where was the fourth coin? It wasn't there. It was _____.

3. Marie's mother saw three coins on the table. One coin was missing, but she didn't pay attention. She didn't _____ that the coin was missing.

4. Marie got sick. She _____, and she couldn't speak.

5. Why couldn't Marie speak? The doctors didn't know, so they took an X-ray of her _____.

3 COMPREHENSION

UNDERSTANDING THE MAIN IDEAS

Circle the letter of the best answer.

1. Marie didn't speak because
   a. a coin was in her throat.
   b. she didn't want to.
   c. a doctor said, "We can't help her."

2. Now Marie can
   a. work again.
   b. bake cakes.
   c. speak again.

REMEMBERING DETAILS

One word in each sentence is not correct. Find the word and cross it out. Write the correct word.

Australian
1. Marie Orr, a 13-year-old ~~French~~ girl, was happy.

2. Her mother was making a special pie for dessert.

3. Marie's mother put four small spoons into the cake for good luck.

4. After breakfast Marie and her family ate the cake.

5. They found three coins in the cake and put them on the floor.

6. The sixth coin was missing, but Marie's mother didn't notice.

7. For 12 days, Marie didn't speak.

8. When she was 25 years old, Marie coughed up the cake, and she could speak again.

UNDERSTANDING A SUMMARY

Imagine this: You want to tell the story "The Coin" to a friend. You want to tell the story quickly, in only four sentences. Which four sentences tell the story best? Check (✓) your answer.

☐ 1. Many Australians put coins in their Christmas cakes for good luck. Marie's mother put four small coins in her cake; then she baked it. After dinner Marie and her family ate the cake. They found three coins in the cake and put them on the table.

☐ 2. When she was 13 years old, Marie ate a piece of cake with a coin in it. The coin stayed in Marie's throat, but she didn't know it. She didn't speak for 12 years. When she was 25 years old, she coughed up the coin, and she could speak again.

4 DISCUSSION

In Australia many people put coins in their Christmas cakes; it is a good-luck custom.

Think about these questions. Talk about good-luck customs with your classmates.

1. What are some good-luck customs in your family or from your native country?

2. Do good-luck customs really bring good luck?

3. Do you have a story about a good-luck custom?

5 WRITING

Marie liked Christmas very much. It was her favorite holiday.

A Answer the questions.

1. What is your favorite holiday?

_____

2. Christmas is in December. When is your favorite holiday?

_____

3. Red and green are the colors for Christmas in the United States. Does your favorite holiday have special colors? What are they?

_____

4. Marie's mother made a cake for dessert. Do you eat anything special on your favorite holiday? What do you eat?

_____

_____

5. Marie's mother put coins in the cake. That was special; she did that only at Christmas. What special things do you do on your favorite holiday?

_____

_____

_____

_____

B Take turns reading the sentences you wrote to a partner. Tell your partner a little more about your favorite holiday.

UNIT 10

1 PRE-READING

A Look at the picture. Answer the questions.

1. Do you have a favorite team? Do you like to watch your team play on TV?

2. Imagine this: There is an important game on TV, and your team is playing. You also have an invitation to go to a party. Do you go to the party, or do you watch the game?

B Read the title of the story. Look at the picture again. Answer the questions.

1. What do you think this story is about?

2. Can you guess what happens?

Love or Baseball?

Joe Vitelli was excited. He liked to watch baseball, and his favorite team was going to play Saturday night. It was a championship game—the biggest game of the year. He was thinking about the game. "Maybe I'll invite some friends to my apartment," he thought. "We can eat pizza and watch the game on TV." Then the phone rang. It was Joe's girlfriend.

"Hi!" she said. "I bought my dress today."

"Your dress?" Joe asked.

"Yes, the dress for the dance," she answered. "Remember? You're taking me to the dance Saturday night."

"Oh, no," Joe thought. "I forgot: The dance is Saturday night."

"Joe?" his girlfriend asked. "You're taking me to the dance, right?"

"Right!" Joe said. "See you Saturday night."

What bad luck! The baseball game and the dance were on the same night! Joe didn't want to go to the dance. He wanted to watch the baseball game. The next day, he called his girlfriend.

"I'm sorry," he told her. "I can't go dancing Saturday night. Today I was playing football, and I broke my leg."

"Oh, no! Poor Joe!" his girlfriend said.

On Saturday night, Joe's girlfriend went to the dance alone, and he watched the baseball game on TV. It was a great game, and his team won. But now Joe had a problem. He and his girlfriend went to the same small university, and he saw her almost every day. A broken leg is in a cast. Joe didn't really have a broken leg, so his leg wasn't in a cast.

Joe bought a big white bandage and put it on his leg. Then he rented a wheelchair. Every day a friend pushed him in the wheelchair from his apartment to the university. For two weeks, Joe's plan worked perfectly. Then he got caught.

He went shopping without his bandage and without his wheelchair. He was walking through the store when his girlfriend saw him.

Joe doesn't have a girlfriend anymore. Now he has a lot of time to watch baseball games, and he is free every Saturday night.

2 VOCABULARY

Complete the sentences with the words below.

almost	cast	got caught	championship	rent

1. The baseball game was important because it was a ___championship___ game.

2. Joe saw his girlfriend on Mondays, Wednesdays, Thursdays, Fridays, and Saturdays. He saw her _____ every day.

3. Joe didn't break his leg. When you really break your leg, the doctors put it in a _____ so that it cannot move.

4. Joe didn't want to buy a wheelchair, so he paid $20 every week to _____ a wheelchair.

5. Joe's girlfriend saw him at the store and thought, "He doesn't really have a broken leg!" Joe _____.

3 COMPREHENSION

UNDERSTANDING WORD GROUPS

Read each group of words. One word in each group doesn't belong. Find the word and cross it out.

said	championship	cast	Saturday night
~~thought~~	team	broken leg	the next day
answered	shopping	bandage	perfectly
told	play	pizza	today
asked	game	wheelchair	every day

REVIEWING THE STORY

Complete each sentence. Then read the story again and check your answers.

Joe was excited because his favorite baseball _____team_____ was going to play
                                               1.

Saturday night. His girlfriend wanted to go to a _____ Saturday night. He
                                                    2.

called her and said, "I'm sorry. I can't take you dancing because I broke my

_____."
        3.

Now Joe had a problem. A broken leg is in a _____. He put a big white
                                              4.

_____ on his leg, and he rented a _____.
        5.   6.

One day, Joe went shopping _____ his bandage and wheelchair. His
                                7.

girlfriend saw him. Now Joe has a lot of time to watch baseball games because he doesn't

have a _____ anymore.
              8.

UNDERSTANDING TIME RELATIONSHIPS

Complete the sentences. Write the letter of the answer on the line.

1. The baseball game and the dance were __c__   a. for two weeks.

2. Joe called his girlfriend and said, "I broke my leg _____   b. every Saturday night.

3. Joe and his girlfriend went to the same university, and he saw   c. on Saturday night.
   her _____
                                                          d. today."
4. Joe's plan worked perfectly _____
                                                          e. almost every day.
5. Now Joe is free _____

4 WRITING/DISCUSSION

Joe liked to watch baseball. How about you? What do you like to do?

A Complete only the first part of each sentence. Write about different things you like to do. For example:

I like to *play soccer* _____, and so does _____.

1. I like to _____, and so does _____.

2. I like to _____, and so does _____.

3. I like to _____, and so does _____.

4. I like to _____, and so does _____.

B Walk around the room and find people who like to do what you like to do. (You will need to ask, "Do you like to...?") Write their names on the lines above to complete each sentence. For example:

I like to *play soccer* _____, and so does *José Luis* _____.

1 PRE-READING

A Look at the picture. Answer the questions.

1. What is this woman doing?

2. Is this a difficult job to do? Why?

B Read the title of the story. Look at the picture again. Answer the questions.

1. What do you think this story is about?

2. Can you guess what happens?

The First Day

It was Crystal Morrow's first day at work as a 911 operator. She was a little nervous.

She sat down at her desk, and a few minutes later, the first call came in. A house was on fire. Crystal sent a fire truck.

The second call came in. There was a robbery. Crystal sent the police.

The third call was a medical emergency. A man was having chest pain. Crystal sent an ambulance.

The fourth call was about a car accident. There were injuries. Crystal sent an ambulance and the police.

During the next four hours, there were 40 more calls. Crystal did her job well. She began to relax.

Then the next call came in.

The call was from a woman. "I'm here with my brother," the woman said. "He has diabetes, and I think he's in diabetic shock. When he talks, he doesn't make sense."

Crystal recognized the woman's voice. It was her aunt. The man with diabetes was Crystal's father.

For a few seconds, Crystal froze. She couldn't talk. She couldn't move. Then she started doing her job. In a calm voice, she asked, "Is he awake?"

"Yes, he is," Crystal's aunt answered. She didn't recognize Crystal's voice. She didn't know she was talking to her niece.

"Is he breathing normally?" Crystal asked.

"Yes."

"I'm sending the paramedics to help you now," Crystal said. "Call back if he gets worse, OK?"

"OK."

"All right. The paramedics are on their way."

After the call, Crystal walked away from her desk. Her supervisor followed her. "Are you OK?" the supervisor asked.

Crystal told her supervisor about the call from her aunt. "Go check on your family," the supervisor said. "Come back to work when you're ready."

When Crystal arrived at her aunt's house, the paramedics were there. They were taking care of her father. Twenty minutes later, he was fine.

The next morning, Crystal was back at work. "What calls will come in today?" she wondered. "A fire? A robbery? An accident? A medical emergency?" She didn't know, but she wasn't nervous.

She was ready.

2 VOCABULARY

Complete the sentences with the words below.

| awake | froze | make sense | recognized | worse |

1. When Crystal's father talked, her aunt couldn't understand him. His words
   didn't ___*make sense*___ .

2. Crystal's father was not sleeping. He was _____ .

3. Crystal knew the call was from her aunt. She _____ her aunt's voice.

4. Crystal couldn't talk or move. She _____ .

5. After the paramedics helped Crystal's father, he was better. He
   wasn't _____ .

3 COMPREHENSION

UNDERSTANDING CAUSE AND EFFECT

Find the best way to complete each sentence. Write the letter of the answer on the line.

1. Crystal was excited and nervous because __d__
2. Crystal began to relax because _____
3. Crystal froze because _____
4. Crystal's supervisor asked, "Are you OK?" because _____
5. Crystal's father was fine in 20 minutes because _____

a. she was doing her job well.
b. the paramedics took care of him.
c. she walked away from her desk.
d. it was her first day at work.
e. the man with diabetes was her father.

REMEMBERING INFORMATION

Read the list of emergencies. What did Crystal send? Write the letter or letters of your answer on the line. (You can write one or two letters.)

a. a fire truck	b. the police	c. an ambulance

1. a man in diabetic shock __c__
2. a house on fire _____
3. a car accident with injuries _____
4. a man with chest pain _____
5. a robbery _____

4 DISCUSSION / WRITING

Crystal will always remember her first day as a 911 operator. How many "firsts" do you remember in your life?

A Read the list of "firsts" below. Check (✓) YES or NO.

Do you remember...	YES	NO
1. your first job?	☐	☐
2. your first car?	☐	☐
3. your first pet?	☐	☐
4. your first plane trip?	☐	☐
5. your first apartment?	☐	☐
6. your first day of school?	☐	☐
7. the first time you voted?	☐	☐
8. the birth of your first child?	☐	☐
9. your baby's first words?	☐	☐
10. your first trip to another country?	☐	☐

Do you remember...

		YES	NO
11.	the first time you rode a horse?	☐	☐
12.	your first suit or party dress?	☐	☐
13.	the first concert you attended?	☐	☐
14.	your first serious boyfriend or girlfriend?	☐	☐
15.	the first time you saw your husband or wife?	☐	☐
16.	the first time you cooked something delicious?	☐	☐
17.	the first time you fixed something that was broken?	☐	☐

B Choose *one* of the "firsts" you remember well. Write 3–5 sentences about it on the lines below. Then share your writing in a small group. Here, for example, is what one student wrote.

I remember my first car.
It was a used car.
It was old, and it was white.
I didn't know how to drive, but I drove it.
I crashed into a light post.

UNIT 12

1 PRE-READING

A Look at the picture. Answer the questions.

1. What is the person doing?

2. Do you have a lottery game in your country? How much can you win?

3. Do you play the lottery? Do you win sometimes?

B Read the title of the story. Look at the picture again. Answer the questions.

1. What do you think this story is about?

2. Can you guess what happens?

The Winning Ticket

Therese Costabile is a cashier at a big drugstore in Cupertino, California. People can buy medicine at the drugstore. They can buy makeup, shampoo, watches, candy, and many other things, too. They pay Ms. Costabile for the things they buy.

At the drugstore, people can also buy tickets for the California State Lottery. They pay one dollar for a lottery ticket. After they buy their tickets, they can see immediately if they are "instant winners" or not. Most people win nothing. Some people win $2. A few lucky people win thousands of dollars.

One day Ms. Costabile was working at the drugstore. She sold three lottery tickets to a woman. The woman looked at the tickets. Then she threw the tickets on the counter and walked away. "These are losing tickets," she thought.

Ms. Costabile picked up the tickets and looked at them. She was surprised. Then she was excited. One ticket was a winning ticket!

"Excuse me!" Ms. Costabile called to the woman. "One of these tickets is a winning ticket. You won $50,000!"

The woman walked back to the counter. She took the winning ticket and looked at it. "You're right," she said. "I won $50,000." The woman walked away slowly, in shock. Then she turned around. "Thanks," she said to Ms. Costabile.

Why did Ms. Costabile tell the woman about the winning ticket? Why didn't she keep it? Didn't she want the $50,000?

"Of course I wanted the money," Ms. Costabile said. "But it was her ticket. It wasn't my ticket."

Ms. Costabile called her mother and told her about the ticket.

"Well, I'm sorry that you aren't rich," her mother said. "But I'm happy that you're honest."

2 VOCABULARY

Complete the sentences with the words below.

cashier	counter	drugstore	lottery ticket	won

1. People buy medicine at a _____*drugstore*_____ .

2. When you buy something at a store, you pay the _____ .

3. The cashier stands behind a high table. The high table is a _____ .

4. People buy a _____ because they want to win money.

5. The state of California will give the woman $50,000 because she _____ the money in the lottery.

3 COMPREHENSION

UNDERSTANDING WORD GROUPS

Read each group of words. One word in each group doesn't belong. Find the word and cross it out.

pay	potatoes	win	happy
counter	medicine	lottery	excited
~~weather~~	makeup	ticket	sick
cashier	shampoo	diet	lucky

REMEMBERING DETAILS

One word in each sentence is not correct. Find the word and cross it out. Write the correct word.

1. Therese Costabile is a ~~manager~~ *cashier* at a big drugstore.

2. She sold three movie tickets to a woman.

3. The woman threw the tickets on the floor and walked away.

4. Ms. Costabile picked up the woman's money and looked at them.

5. Ms. Costabile called to the woman, "You won $5!"

6. The woman took the winning ticket and walked away slowly, in anger.

7. Ms. Costabile told her uncle about the winning ticket.

8. Her mother said, "Well, I'm sorry that you aren't rich, but I'm happy that you're friendly."

UNDERSTANDING CAUSE AND EFFECT

Find the best way to complete each sentence. Write the letter of the answer on the line.

1. People pay Therese Costabile __c__

2. The woman threw the tickets on the counter _____

3. Ms. Costabile didn't keep the winning ticket _____

4. Ms. Costabile's mother was happy _____

a. because it wasn't her ticket.

b. because her daughter is honest.

c. because she is a cashier.

d. because she thought they were losing tickets.

4 DISCUSSION

The woman in the story took the winning ticket from Ms. Costabile and kept the $50,000 for herself.

A Imagine this: You are the woman in the story. Ms. Costabile tells you that you have a winning ticket. You won $50,000! What do you do next? Check (✓) your answer.

You...

☐ 1. say "thank you" and walk away.

☐ 2. give her half the money—$25,000.

☐ 3. give her $_____ .

☐ 4. _____
(Write your own idea.)

B Discuss your answer with your classmates.

5 WRITING

A Imagine this: You win $50,000 in the lottery. What will you do with the money? Will you buy a car, go on a vacation, buy presents for everyone you know? Make a list of things you will buy or do.

With my $50,000, I will...

_____

_____

_____

_____

_____

_____

_____

_____

B Read your list to a partner. Tell your partner why you want to buy or do the things on your list.

UNIT 13

1 PRE-READING

A Look at the picture. Answer the questions.

1. What animal is this?

2. Is this an intelligent animal? Why or why not?

B Read the title of the story. Look at the picture again. Answer the questions.

1. What do you think this story is about?

2. Can you guess what happens?

Thank You

One morning a fisherman was fishing in the Pacific Ocean, about 18 miles from San Francisco. He saw something strange. There was a whale in the water, and it wasn't moving. Was the whale dead? The fisherman didn't think so. He moved his boat to take a closer look.

The whale wasn't dead. It was caught in fishing lines, and it couldn't move. It was a special whale—a humpback whale. There are only 6,000 humpback whales in the world. The fisherman called for help.

A few hours later, five men from San Francisco arrived to help. From their boat, they looked at the whale. They saw fishing lines everywhere. The fishing lines were around the whale's body, around its tail, and in its mouth. "We have to go into the water," the men said. "We have to cut the fishing lines."

The men looked at one another. The whale was very big, and it was dangerous. "If the whale moves its tail, it will kill us," they said.

"I'll go in the water," one man said. "I'll go in, too," a second man said. "Me too," a third man said. "Me too," a fourth man said. The four men put on diving suits and jumped into the water. Each man held a knife in his hand. A fifth man, the captain of the boat, stayed in the boat.

The men began cutting the fishing lines. The whale watched them. One man was near the whale's eye. He saw the whale blink. But the whale didn't move.

One hour later, the men cut the last fishing line. The whale swam away. It swam in big circles and jumped into the air. Then it swam back to the men. Why was it swimming back? What was it going to do? The men in the water were afraid to move.

The whale swam to the first man and stopped. It pushed him gently with its nose. Then it swam to the second man, and the third man, and the fourth man. It pushed each man gently with its nose. Was the whale thanking the men? They thought so. They touched the whale with their hands and rubbed against it with their shoulders. "You're welcome," they told the whale. "You're very welcome."

2 VOCABULARY

Which words or pictures have the same meaning as the words in *italics*? Circle the letter of the answer.

1. Fishing lines were around the whale's *tail*.

2. The man is wearing a *diving suit*.

   a.    b.

3. The whale *blinked*.
   a. closed its mouth and then opened it
   b. closed its eye and then opened it

4. Each man rubbed against the whale with his *shoulder*.

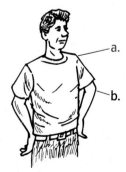

3 PRACTICING PRONUNCIATION

The underlined words are in the story. If you can say them correctly, you can say the
words below them correctly, too. Practice with your teacher.

<u>hand</u>	<u>each</u>	<u>swam</u>	<u>stay</u>	<u>will</u>	<u>dead</u>
band	beach	slam	day	bill	bread
land	peach	spam	pay	fill	head
sand	reach	ham	play	kill	read (past tense)
stand	teach	jam	pray	pill	spread

4 COMPREHENSION

UNDERSTANDING THE MAIN IDEAS

Circle the letter of the correct answer.

1. The fisherman moved his boat because
   a. he wanted to take a closer look at the whale.
   b. he was afraid of the whale.

2. The whale couldn't move because
   a. it was sick.
   b. it was caught in fishing lines.

3. Humpback whales are special because
   a. they are very big.
   b. there are only 6,000 in the world.

4. The men from San Francisco had to go into the water because
   a. they needed to take a closer look at the whale.
   b. they needed to cut the fishing lines.

5. The whale was dangerous because
   a. it could kill the men with its tail.
   b. it had very big teeth.

6. The whale swam back to the men because
   a. it wanted to thank them.
   b. it wanted food.

UNDERSTANDING A SUMMARY

Imagine this: You want to tell the story "Thank You" to a friend. You want to tell the story
quickly, in only five sentences. Which five sentences tell the story best? Check (✓) your answer.

☐ 1. A humpback whale was caught in fishing lines. Four men jumped into the water and
      cut the lines. The whale swam away, but then swam back to the men. It pushed each
      man gently with its nose. It was saying "Thank you."

☐ 2. A fisherman was fishing in the Pacific Ocean about 18 miles from San Francisco.
      He saw a humpback whale in the water. The whale wasn't moving. It was caught in
      fishing lines. The fisherman called for help.

5 DISCUSSION / WRITING

A In a small group, guess the answers to the questions about the humpback whale. Your group must decide on one answer to each question. Write short answers on the lines. Then look in the Key to Guessed Answers on page 91. Were your group's guesses correct?

1. What color are humpback whales? *black and white*

2. What do they eat? _____

3. How many kilograms of food does a humpback whale eat every day? _____

4. How many months is a female humpback whale pregnant? _____

5. How many kilograms does a baby humpback whale weigh when it is born? _____

6. What does a baby humpback whale eat during its first year of life? _____

B Write the correct answers to the questions above. Write your answers in complete sentences. The first one is done for you.

1. *They are black and white.*

2. _____

3. _____

4. _____

5. _____

6. _____

UNIT 14

The Lorenzo family

1 PRE-READING

A **Look at the picture. Answer the questions.**

1. Where do you think the Lorenzo family is from?

2. Can you guess how they feel and why?

B **Read the title of the story. Look at the picture again. Answer the questions.**

1. What do you think this story is about?

2. Can you guess what happens?

Together Again

Orestes Lorenzo was a pilot in the Cuban Air Force. Orestes liked the Air Force and he liked flying, but he didn't like living in Cuba. He didn't like the political system. Orestes wanted to live in the United States, but the Cuban government told him, "No. You can't leave Cuba."

In March of 1991, Orestes got into a Cuban Air Force jet and flew the jet to Florida. "I'm never going back to Cuba," he thought.

When Orestes flew to the United States, he left his wife and two sons in Cuba. Orestes thought, "My family can come to the United States later."

Orestes was wrong. The Cuban government told Orestes's wife, "You can't leave Cuba. Forget your husband."

For almost two years, Orestes lived in the United States, and his family lived in Cuba. Orestes was very unhappy. In Cuba he had his family, but he didn't like the political system. In the United States, he liked the political system, but he didn't have his family.

One day Orestes got a letter from his son Alejandro. "Dear Daddy," Alejandro wrote. "You are a pilot. Fly to Cuba! Take us to the United States in an airplane!"

Orestes read Alejandro's letter and began to think. "Maybe Alejandro has a good idea," he thought. "Maybe I can fly to Cuba and get my family."

Orestes wrote a letter to his wife, Victoria. In the letter, Orestes told Victoria, "On December 19 at 5:30 p.m., take the boys to our favorite beach for a picnic. Wear orange T-shirts. And watch the sky."

At 5:30 on December 19, Victoria and the two boys were at the beach. The boys were playing, but Victoria was watching the sky. She saw a small plane. It was flying low over a highway nearby. "Run to the highway!" she told the boys. "It's Daddy!"

Orestes was flying a small plane right over the highway. He flew over a car, a bus, and a truck. Then he landed on the highway. Victoria and the boys got into the plane, and the plane took off. Fifty minutes later, the Lorenzo family was in Florida.

Later Victoria said, "I knew he would come. I always knew it. I believe in him. I believe in love."

2 VOCABULARY

Which words or pictures have the same meaning as the words in *italics*? Circle the letter of the answer.

1. Orestes flew a *jet* to Florida.
   a. a fast airplane
   b. a small airplane

2. Orestes flew low over the *highway*.
   a. a big road between two cities
   b. a small street in a city

3. Orestes *landed* on the highway.

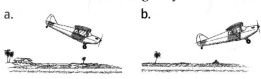

   a.   b.

4. Victoria and the boys got into the plane, and the plane *took off*.

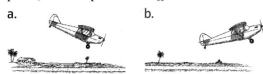

   a.   b.

3 COMPREHENSION

FINDING INFORMATION

There are two correct ways to complete each sentence below and one incorrect way. Circle the letters of the two correct answers.

1. In Cuba, Orestes liked
   - **(a.)** flying.
   - **b.** his house.
   - **(c.)** the Air Force.

2. When Orestes flew to Florida, he thought,
   - **a.** "The U.S. Air Force wants this jet."
   - **b.** "I'm never going back to Cuba."
   - **c.** "My family can come to the United States later."

3. The Cuban government told Orestes's wife,
   - **a.** "You can't leave Cuba."
   - **b.** "Forget your husband."
   - **c.** "Your husband is dead."

4. After he read Alejandro's letter, Orestes thought,
   - **a.** "Maybe Alejandro has a good idea."
   - **b.** "I miss my son very much."
   - **c.** "Maybe I can fly to Cuba and get my family."

5. In his letter to Victoria, Orestes wrote,
   - **a.** "I bought a small plane."
   - **b.** "Take the boys to our favorite beach for a picnic."
   - **c.** "Wear orange T-shirts."

MAKING CONNECTIONS

Find the best way to complete each sentence. Write the letter of the answer on the line.

1. Orestes thought, "My family can come to the United States later," but ___*b*___

2. In Cuba, Orestes had his family, but _____

3. In the United States, Orestes liked the political system, but _____

4. On December 19, the boys were playing on the beach, but _____

a. he didn't like the political system.

b. the Cuban government told Orestes's wife, "You can't leave Cuba."

c. Victoria was watching the sky.

d. he didn't have his family.

REMEMBERING DETAILS

One word in each sentence is not correct. Find the word and cross it out. Write the correct word.

1. Orestes Lorenzo was a ~~mechanic~~ *pilot* in the Cuban Air Force.

2. Orestes got into a Cuban Air Force jet and flew the jet to California.

3. When Orestes flew to Florida, he left his wife and two daughters in Cuba.

4. For almost ten years, Orestes lived in the United States, and his family lived in Cuba.

5. Orestes landed a small plane on a beach in Cuba.

4 WRITING / DISCUSSION

Orestes Lorenzo liked living in the United States because he liked the political system. He didn't like living in the United States because he didn't have his family.

A Are you living in the United States? What do you like about it? What don't you like? Make two lists.

IN THE UNITED STATES

I like...   I don't like...

_____   _____

_____   _____

_____   _____

_____   _____

B What about your native country? What do you like about it? What don't you like? Make two lists.

IN MY NATIVE COUNTRY

I like...   I don't like...

_____   _____

_____   _____

_____   _____

_____   _____

C Take turns reading your lists to a partner. Are your lists and your partner's lists the same?

UNIT **15**

1 PRE-READING

A Look at the picture. Answer the questions.

1. Where are these people? What are they doing?

2. Are they doing something dangerous?

B Read the title of the story. Look at the picture again. Answer the questions.

1. What do you think this story is about?

2. Can you guess what happens?

Saved by the Bell

Nevado del Ruiz is a mountain in Colombia. It is 5,425 meters high, and it is popular with climbers. It is beautiful, but it is dangerous, too. The weather can change quickly on the mountain. One minute it is sunny, and the next minute it is cloudy. One minute it is warm, and the next minute it is cold.

On a sunny morning in June, Leonardo Diaz began climbing Nevado del Ruiz with some friends. On the second day of their climb, there was a snowstorm. It was difficult to walk in the snow, and it was difficult to see. The climbers decided to turn around and walk down the mountain. Leonardo stopped for a minute to get something out of his backpack. When he looked up, his friends were gone. He couldn't see them or their footprints in the snow. "Wait!" Leonardo shouted. But his friends couldn't hear him in the storm.

All day Leonardo continued down the mountain alone. That night he put up his tent, crawled inside, and slept. When he woke up the next morning, he was in big trouble. His clothes were not warm enough, so he was very cold. He was hungry, too, because he had no food left. He decided to call for help. He opened his backpack and took out his cell phone. It didn't work.

Leonardo had no more prepaid minutes on his phone.

All morning Leonardo stayed in his tent and listened to the storm. He began to think, "Maybe I'll die on this mountain."

Then his cell phone rang.

"Hello?" he answered.

"Good afternoon," a woman said. "I'm calling from Bell South Phone Company. You have no minutes left on your cell phone. Would you like to buy more minutes?"

"Yes!" Leonardo shouted into the phone. "Please help me! I'm lost in a snowstorm on Nevado del Ruiz."

"Excuse me," the woman said. "I don't understand. Do you want to buy more minutes?"

"Yes, but not now!" Leonardo said. "I need help. I'm lost on a mountain."

"Stay where you are," the woman said. "I'll send for help."

Late that night, a rescue team arrived and helped Leonardo down the mountain.

Leonardo says he will probably try again to climb Nevado del Ruiz. But the next time, he will bring plenty of warm clothes and plenty of food. He will also bring a cell phone with plenty of prepaid minutes.

2 VOCABULARY

Complete the sentences with the words below.

crawled	plenty	shouted	trouble

1. Leonardo's tent was small, so Leonardo went inside on his hands and knees. He
   _____*crawled*_____ into his tent.

2. Leonardo was lost in a snowstorm. He was cold and hungry, too. He was in
   big _____ .

3. Leonardo spoke loudly when he talked on the phone. "Help me!" he _____ .

4. The next time Leonardo climbs the mountain, he will bring two jackets, a hat, and gloves.
   He will bring _____ of warm clothes.

3 COMPREHENSION

REMEMBERING DETAILS

Read the summary of the story "Saved by the Bell." There are ten mistakes in the summary. Find the mistakes and cross them out. Write the correct words. The first one is done for you.

On a ~~cloudy~~ *sunny* morning in July, Leonardo and his family began climbing Nevado del

Ruiz, a mountain in Peru. On the second day of their climb, they decided to turn around

because there was a rainstorm. Leonardo stopped to get something out of his pocket.

When he looked up, his friends were gone.

Leonardo was lost on the mountain. He tried to call for help on his radio, but it didn't

work. He didn't have any more prepaid hours. He stayed in his tent and waited for the

storm to stop. Then his cell phone rang. A man from the phone company asked Leonardo,

"Do you want to buy more minutes for your cell phone?" Leonardo asked her for help,

and she sent a ski team. They helped Leonardo down the mountain.

UNDERSTANDING DIALOGUE

A Below is the conversation between Leonardo and the woman from the phone company. Some words are missing from their conversation. Write the missing words on the lines.

A: Hello?

B: Good afternoon. I'm calling from Bell South Phone Company. Would you like to buy

more minutes for your _____*cell*_____ phone?

A: Yes! Please help me! I'm _____ in a snowstorm on Nevado del Ruiz.

B: Excuse me. I don't understand. Do you want to buy more _____?

A: Yes, but not now! I need _____. I'm lost on a mountain.

B: _____ where you are. I'll send for help.

B Practice the conversation with a partner. One student is speaker A, and the other student is speaker B.

Read each sentence on the left. Which sentence on the right gives you more information?
Write the letter of the answer on the line.

_c_ 1. Nevado del Ruiz is a mountain in
Colombia.

a. One minute it is warm, and the next
minute it is cold.

_____ 2. The weather can change quickly on
the mountain.

b. He couldn't see them or their footprints.

c. It is 5,425 meters high.

_____ 3. There was a snowstorm.

d. It had no more prepaid minutes.

_____ 4. Leonardo's friends were gone.

e. It was difficult to walk, and it was
difficult to see.

_____ 5. Leonardo's cell phone didn't work.

4 DISCUSSION

Leonardo was not prepared for an emergency on the mountain. He didn't have warm
clothes, he didn't have enough food, and he didn't have any prepaid minutes left on his
cell phone.

Are *you* prepared for an emergency? With your classmates, make a list of things you need
in your home for an emergency (a flashlight, for example). Which things do you have? Tell
the class.

5 WRITING

The weather on Nevado del Ruiz can be warm or cold, sunny or cloudy. How is the weather
in your native city?

Write a few sentences about each season in your native country. Here is what one
student wrote.

*In the fall, it is very beautiful. The temperature is usually
20 degrees Celsius, and the sky is clear. When the trees change to
beautiful colors, we go to the mountains for picnics.*

In the winter, _____

_____

In the spring, _____

_____

In the summer, _____

_____

In the fall, _____

_____

UNIT 16

Walter Polovchak at age 12

Walter Polovchak as an adult

1 PRE-READING

A **Look at the pictures. Answer the questions.**

1. Walter Polovchak was born in Ukraine. Where do you think he lives now?

2. How do you think he felt at age 12?

3. How do you think he feels as an adult?

B **Read the title of the story. Look at the pictures again. Answer the questions.**

1. What do you think this story is about?

2. Can you guess what happens?

This Is the Place for Me

Walter Polovchak, a 12-year-old boy, was listening to rock 'n' roll music. "Turn off that garbage!" his father shouted. Walter turned off the music.

Walter and his family lived in Chicago, Illinois, but they were from Ukraine. Walter's father wasn't happy in Chicago. He didn't like American rock 'n' roll. He didn't like his job. He didn't like the weather. He didn't like the food or water. "Coming to the United States was a big mistake," Walter's father said. "We're going back home."

Walter didn't want to leave Chicago. He liked his school, and he liked American sports. He liked American food, too. Walter was happy in the United States. His 18-year-old sister Natalie was happy, too. Walter and Natalie packed their clothes and went to live with a cousin. "We're not going back to Ukraine," they said.

Walter's parents said, "Natalie is 18. She can stay in the United States. But Walter is only 12. He has to come with us." Walter's parents called the police. "We want our son," they told the police. The police didn't know what to do. They called U.S. immigration officials. The officials made a decision: Walter could stay in the United States.

Walter's parents went back to Ukraine without Walter and Natalie. But first they hired a lawyer. "We want our son," they told the lawyer. "Go to court. Help us get our son back."

The U.S. courts said, "Walter's parents are right. The immigration officials were wrong. Walter has to go back to Ukraine." But Walter didn't go back. When the court finally made its decision, Walter Polovchak was 18 years old. He was an adult, so he could live where he wanted to live. He stayed in the United States.

Walter Polovchak is in his 50s now. He is married, has two sons, and still lives in Chicago. His parents lived in Ukraine for the rest of their lives. Walter and his family visited them often. He is sorry they lived far away, but he is not sorry he stayed in the United States. "I couldn't go back to Ukraine," he says. "In my heart, I always knew that this was the place for me."

2 VOCABULARY

Which sentence has the same meaning as the sentence with the words or phrases in *italics*? Circle the letter of the answer.

1. Walter was listening to rock 'n' roll music. His father didn't like rock 'n' roll. *"Turn off that garbage!" he shouted.*
   a. "Turn off that beautiful music!" he said quietly.
   b. "Turn off that terrible music!" he said loudly.

2. Walter and Natalie *packed their clothes* and went to live with a cousin.
   a. Walter and Natalie put their clothes in a suitcase.
   b. Walter and Natalie gave their clothes to their parents.

3. Walter's parents went back to Ukraine *without* Walter and Natalie.
   a. Walter's parents went back to Ukraine. Walter and Natalie went back to Ukraine, too.
   b. Walter's parents went back to Ukraine. Walter and Natalie stayed in the United States.

4. Walter's parents *hired* a lawyer.
   a. Walter's parents told the lawyer, "Work for us. We will pay you."
   b. Walter's parents told the lawyer, "We don't need your help. Please go away."

3 COMPREHENSION

FINDING INFORMATION

There are two correct ways to complete each sentence below and one incorrect way. Circle the letters of the two correct answers.

1. The Polovchak family
   - (a.) was from Ukraine.
   - b. had a lot of money.
   - (c.) lived in Chicago.

2. Walter's father
   - a. wasn't happy in Chicago.
   - b. wanted to go back home.
   - c. was 45 years old.

3. Walter
   - a. was a good student.
   - b. was 12 years old.
   - c. didn't want to leave Chicago.

4. Walter's parents wanted their son back, so they
   - a. gave him many gifts.
   - b. called the police.
   - c. hired a lawyer.

5. Today, Walter Polovchak
   - a. has a good job.
   - b. is in his 50s.
   - c. still lives in Chicago.

UNDERSTANDING CAUSE AND EFFECT

Find the best way to complete each sentence. Write the letter of the answer on the line.

1. Walter's father wasn't happy in Chicago, so __b__

2. Walter and Natalie didn't want to go back to Ukraine, so _____

3. Walter's parents said, "Natalie is 18, so _____

4. When the court finally made its decision, Walter was 18, so _____

a. she can stay in the United States."

b. he said, "We're going back to Ukraine."

c. he could live where he wanted to live.

d. they packed their clothes and went to live with a cousin.

LOOKING FOR DETAILS

A What didn't Walter's father like? Find the words in the story.

American rock 'n' roll _____ _____

_____ _____

_____

B What did Walter like? Find the words in the story.

his school _____   _____

_____

4 DISCUSSION

After six months in the United States, Walter's father wanted to go back to Ukraine. He was not happy in Chicago. That is not unusual. When people arrive in a new country, they are usually happy. A few weeks or a few months later, many people are sad. After one or two years in the new country, they are usually OK.

A   Are you in a new country now? How do you feel? Happy? Sad? OK? Going down? Coming up? Where are you now? Put an *X* on the line.

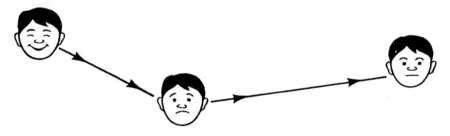

B   Show a partner where you put your *X*. Why did you put your *X* there? Tell your partner.

5 WRITING

A   Imagine you are Walter's father. You are living in the United States. Answer the questions. Complete the sentences.

1. How did you feel when you arrived? (Excited? Sad? Afraid? Nervous?)

   When I came here, I felt _____ because _____

   _____ .

2. How do you feel now?

   Now I feel _____ because _____

   _____ .

3. How will you feel in one year?

   Maybe I will feel _____ because _____

   _____ .

B   Are you in a new country now? Answer the same questions and complete the sentences about yourself.

1 PRE-READING

A Look at the picture. Answer the questions.

1. What happens at a wedding in your country?

2. What happens after the wedding? Is there a party? A dinner? Music?

3. Where is the woman? Why do you think she feels sad?

B Read the title of the story. Look at the picture again. Answer the questions.

1. What do you think this story is about?

2. Can you guess what happens?

Nicole's Party

On the morning of her wedding day, Nicole Contos got a phone call from her fiancé. His name was Tasos. "I love you, Nicole," Tasos said. "But I'm really nervous. My legs are like jelly."

"I'm a little nervous, too," Nicole said. "Don't worry. Everything will be fine. I love you, too."

That afternoon Nicole put on her white wedding dress and went to a church in New York City. At the church, she held a bouquet of flowers in her hands and waited.

At the front of the church, a minister stood and waited.

In the church, 250 guests sat quietly. They were the friends and family of Nicole and Tasos. They waited, too.

Everyone was waiting for Tasos. They waited, and waited, and waited.

Finally, Tasos's best friend walked into the church. "Tasos isn't coming," he whispered to Nicole's brother. "He doesn't want to get married. He changed his mind."

Nicole's brother told Nicole that Tasos wasn't coming. First, Nicole cried. Then she thought about the wedding guests. At a hotel near the church, ten cooks were making dinner for them, and a band was getting ready to play music.

"Tell the guests there isn't going to be a wedding today," Nicole told her brother. "But tell them there *is* going to be a party. Tell them to go to the hotel."

Nicole went home and put on a black party dress. Then she went to the hotel. As the guests ate dinner and wedding cake, Nicole walked from table to table and smiled. "Thank you for coming," she told her guests. After dinner, the band played music. Nicole was the first one on the dance floor. She danced with her brother. Inside, her heart was breaking. But all evening, she never stopped smiling.

Later Nicole said, "I'll be OK. Something good came from this experience: I learned how strong I really am."

At the end of the evening, Nicole's brother raised his glass and said, "Let's all drink to Nicole. She's a great woman. Someday a lucky man will marry her, and she will make him really, really happy."

2 VOCABULARY

Complete the sentences with the words below.

changed his mind	fiancé	guests	wedding	whispered

1. Nicole was going to marry Tasos. He was her _____*fiancé*_____.

2. They were going to get married in New York City. The _____ was at a church.

3. Many people came to see the wedding. They were the wedding _____.

4. Tasos's friend didn't want the minister or the guests to hear what he said. So he spoke quietly. "Tasos isn't coming," he _____.

5. First Tasos said, "I want to marry Nicole." Then he said, "I don't want to marry Nicole." He _____.

3 PRACTICING PRONUNCIATION

The underlined words are in the story. If you can say them correctly, you can say the words below them correctly, too. Practice with your teacher.

day	went	then	tell	cook	make
May	bent	men	cell	book	bake
pay	dent	pen	fell	hook	cake
say	rent	ten	sell	look	lake
way	sent	when	well	took	take

4 COMPREHENSION

UNDERSTANDING THE MAIN IDEAS

Circle the letter of the best answer.

1. On the morning of their wedding day, Tasos called Nicole and said,
   a. "I'm going to be really late."
   b. "I'm really nervous."
   c. "I'm really happy."

2. Tasos didn't come to the church because
   a. he was sick.
   b. he had a car accident.
   c. he didn't want to get married.

3. When Tasos didn't come to the church, Nicole
   a. looked for him all over New York City.
   b. went home and stayed in bed.
   c. cried but then went to the hotel for a party.

4. From her experience, Nicole learned that
   a. she was really strong.
   b. weddings are expensive.
   c. all men are nervous about getting married.

UNDERSTANDING QUOTATIONS

Who said it? Match the sentences and the people. Write the letter of the answer on the line.

_b_ 1. "Let's all drink to Nicole."   a. Nicole

____ 2. "Tasos doesn't want to get married."   b. Nicole's brother

____ 3. "My legs are like jelly."   c. Tasos's best friend

____ 4. "Something good came from this experience."   d. Tasos

5 DISCUSSION

Look at the pictures below. You often see these things at weddings in the United States. Do you see these things at weddings in your native country? Which things are the same? Which are different? Tell the class.

6 WRITING

Write four sentences about weddings in your native country. For example:

Sometimes a wedding lasts for two or three days.
Sometimes many people get married at the same time.

1. _____

2. _____

3. _____

4. _____

1 PRE-READING

A Look at the picture. Answer the questions.

1. Where are these people? What are they doing?

2. Are they doing something that can be dangerous?

B Read the title of the story. Look at the picture again. Answer the questions.

1. What do you think this story is about?

2. Can you guess what happens?

A Strong Little Boy

Chicago, Illinois, is next to a big, beautiful lake—Lake Michigan. In the summer, Lake Michigan is warm and blue. People lie on the beaches and swim in the water. In the winter, Lake Michigan is cold and gray. Snow covers the beaches, and ice covers the water.

On a cold January day, a little boy and his father were playing in the snow on a Chicago beach. The boy was Jimmy Tontlewicz. He was four years old.

Jimmy was playing with a sled. He pushed the sled down a small hill. The sled went onto the ice of Lake Michigan. Jimmy ran after the sled. He ran onto the ice. Suddenly the ice broke, and Jimmy fell into the cold water.

Jimmy's father jumped into the water. He couldn't find Jimmy. Minutes went by. He still couldn't find Jimmy. "My kid is dead! My kid is dead!" he screamed.

Men from the Chicago Fire Department arrived. Twenty minutes later, they found Jimmy and pulled him out of the water. Jimmy was not breathing, and his heart was not beating. He was dead.

At the beach, paramedics worked on Jimmy for one hour. He began to breathe, and his heart began to beat again. The paramedics rushed Jimmy to the hospital.

Doctors at the hospital put Jimmy in bed. They put him on a cold mattress because they wanted his body to warm up slowly. They gave him some medicine because they wanted him to sleep.

After eight days in the hospital, Jimmy woke up, but he couldn't walk or talk. He stayed in the hospital for six weeks. Every day he got better. Then he went to another hospital. He stayed there for seven weeks. He began to walk, talk, and play again.

Jimmy was in the water for over 20 minutes. He couldn't breathe in the water. He couldn't get any oxygen. But today he is alive and healthy. How is it possible?

Jimmy is alive because the water was ice cold. Usually the brain needs a lot of oxygen. But when it's very cold, the brain slows down. It does not need much oxygen. So the ice-cold water saved Jimmy.

Jimmy's father has another reason. He says, "Jimmy is alive today because he is a fighter. He is a strong little boy."

2 VOCABULARY

Which sentence has the same meaning as the sentence with the words or phrases in *italics*? Circle the letter of the answer.

1. Snow covers the beaches, and ice *covers* the water.
   a. Snow is on the beaches, and ice is on the water.
   b. Snow is near the beaches, and ice is near the water.

2. The paramedics *worked on* Jimmy for one hour.
   a. The doctor's assistants helped Jimmy work again. Jimmy worked for one hour.
   b. The doctor's assistants helped Jimmy breathe again. They helped Jimmy for one hour.

3. The paramedics *rushed* Jimmy to the hospital.
   a. The paramedics took Jimmy to the hospital. They drove fast.
   b. The paramedics took Jimmy to the hospital. They drove slowly.

4. Jimmy was in the water for *over 20 minutes*.
   a. Jimmy was in the water for more than 20 minutes.
   b. Jimmy was in the water for 20 minutes.

3 COMPREHENSION

FINDING INFORMATION

Read the questions. Find the answers in the story. Write the answers.

1. Was it a cold day in January or a warm day in May?

   It was a cold day in January.

2. Were Jimmy and his father playing in a Chicago park or on a Chicago beach?

   _____

3. Did Jimmy run onto the ice or into the water?

   _____

4. Did the sled break, or did the ice break?

   _____

5. Who pulled Jimmy out of the water, his father or firefighters?

   _____

6. Was Jimmy in the water for over two minutes or for over 20 minutes?

   _____

UNDERSTANDING CAUSE AND EFFECT

Find the best way to complete each sentence. Write the letter of the answer on the line.

1. Jimmy fell into the cold water __d__

2. Paramedics worked on Jimmy _____

3. Doctors put Jimmy on a cold mattress _____

4. Doctors at the hospital gave Jimmy some medicine _____

5. Jimmy is alive today _____

a. because they wanted Jimmy to warm up slowly.

b. because they wanted Jimmy to sleep.

c. because the water was ice cold.

d. because the ice broke.

e. because they wanted Jimmy to breathe again.

UNDERSTANDING WORD GROUPS

Read each group of words. One word in each group doesn't belong. Find the word and cross it out.

ice	paramedics	alive	mattress
cold	hospital	got better	garden
~~hot~~	pilot	strong	wake up
winter	medicine	healthy	sleep
snow	doctors	nervous	bed

4 DISCUSSION

A Do you have any experience with fire departments, rescues, ambulances, paramedics, or hospitals? With the help of your teacher or your dictionary, read the sentences below and check (✓) *YES* or *NO*.

		YES	NO
1.	I called the fire department.	☐	☐
2.	I called an ambulance.	☐	☐
3.	I saw a rescue.	☐	☐
4.	Someone rescued me.	☐	☐
5.	I saw paramedics. They were working on someone.	☐	☐
6.	Paramedics worked on me.	☐	☐
7.	I went to the hospital in an ambulance.	☐	☐
8.	Someone in my family went to the hospital in an ambulance.	☐	☐
9.	I was a patient in a hospital.	☐	☐
10.	Someone in my family was a patient in a hospital.	☐	☐
11.	I know a true story about a rescue.	☐	☐

B Read your *YES* sentences to a partner. Tell your partner about your experiences.

5 WRITING

When Jimmy was in the hospital, he got cards and letters from people all over the world. "Get well soon," people wrote. "We are thinking of you."

A Imagine this: Your friend is in the hospital. Maybe your friend is sick, or maybe your friend had an accident. What can you write to your friend? Make a list of possible sentences with your classmates. Your teacher will write your sentences on the board.

B On the lines below, write a short letter (two or three sentences) to your friend in the hospital.

_____

_____

_____

_____

_____

Károly Takács

Olympic gold medal

1 PRE-READING

A Look at the pictures. Answer the questions.

1. What Olympic sports are popular in your country?

2. Do you have any Olympic "heroes" in your country? Who are they and what did they do?

3. Karoly Takas won an Olympic gold medal for Hungary. In what sport did he win and when?

B Read the title of the story. Look at the pictures again. Answer the questions.

1. What do you think this story is about?

2. Can you guess what happens?

The Champion

In 1938, before his accident, Károly Takács had big plans. He wanted to be an Olympic champion. He was very good at shooting a pistol, and he was on the Hungarian pistol-shooting team. "Maybe I can win a gold medal at the next Olympics," he thought. Then the accident happened.

Károly was a soldier in the Hungarian army. One day he was practicing with grenades. He picked up a grenade and held it in his hand. Before he could throw it, the grenade exploded. Doctors had to cut off Károly's right hand—his shooting hand.

Károly was in the hospital for a month. Then he went home to rest. He was very depressed. He didn't want to see his friends, and he never went out. He stayed in bed almost all day. His wife was worried about him.

One day Károly came out of the bedroom with a pistol in his left hand. "What are you going to do with the pistol?" his wife asked. Károly didn't answer. He walked toward the door. "Károly, where are you going?" his wife asked. He didn't say anything. He went out the door and walked quickly into the woods behind their house. Károly's wife heard a gunshot in the woods, and she almost fainted. Then she heard another shot, and another, and another. Károly was practicing in the woods. He was learning to shoot with his left hand.

A year later, Károly went to the Hungarian National Pistol-Shooting Competition. When people saw him, they were surprised. "We're sorry about your accident," they told him. "Did you come to watch the competition?"

"No," Károly said. "I came here to shoot." He won the competition. After that, he began to think about the Olympics again.

In 1940 and 1944, there were no Olympic Games because of World War II. So Károly had eight years to practice. In 1948, he went to the Olympics with the Hungarian team. He won the gold medal in pistol shooting. In 1952, he returned to the Olympics and won another gold medal in pistol shooting.

Before his accident, Károly Takács had big plans: He wanted to be an Olympic champion. After his accident, he became an Olympic champion, and more: In Hungary, he was a national hero.

2 VOCABULARY

Complete the sentences with the words below.

army	exploded	happened	hero	medal	pistol

1. Károly Takács was good at shooting a _____*pistol*_____.

2. He was a soldier in the _____.

3. The grenade _____.

4. The accident _____ in 1938.

5. He won an Olympic gold _____.

6. When he returned to Hungary, he was a national _____.

3 COMPREHENSION

UNDERSTANDING WORD GROUPS

Read each group of words. One word in each group doesn't belong. Find the word and cross it out.

grenade	Olympics	hospital	worried
~~fisherman~~	medal	accident	sorry
army	champion	school	depressed
soldier	letter	doctors	excited

FINDING INFORMATION

Read each question. Find the answer in the paragraph below and circle it. Write the number of the question above your answer.

1. Why were there no Olympic Games in 1940 and 1944?
2. How many years did Takács practice for the Olympics?
3. Where did he go in 1948?
4. Who went with him?
5. What did he win there?
6. When did he return to the Olympics?

In 1940 and 1944, there were no Olympic Games (because of World War II.) [1] So Károly

had eight years to practice. In 1948, he went to the Olympics with the Hungarian team.

He won the gold medal in pistol shooting. In 1952, he returned to the Olympics and won

another gold medal in pistol shooting.

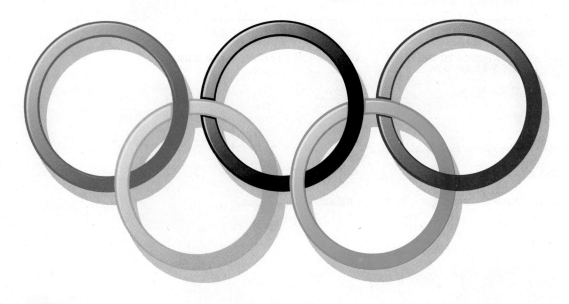

UNDERSTANDING SEQUENCE

When did it happen? Match the dates and the sentences. Write the answer on the line.

- He won his second Olympic gold medal.
- He practiced for the Olympics.
- Takács lost his right hand in a grenade accident.
- He won his first Olympic gold medal.
- He won the Hungarian National Pistol-Shooting Competition.

1938 _Takács lost his right hand in a grenade accident._

1939 _____

1940–1948 _____

1948 _____

1952 _____

4 WRITING / DISCUSSION

Károly Takács is a national hero in Hungary. Who is a national hero in your native country?

A Write about a national hero in your country. Complete the sentence. Here, for example, is what one student wrote.

Juan Santamaría is a national hero in _Costa Rica_ because _he set fire to a hacienda during a battle, and he helped the Costa Rican people win a war_.

_____ is a national hero in _____ because

_____

_____.

B Read your sentence to the class. If you can, tell the class more about the national hero.

UNIT 20

1 PRE-READING

A Look at the picture. Answer the questions.

1. This bottle has a message in it. Why do people sometimes put a message in a bottle and put the bottle in the ocean?

2. How far can a bottle travel in the ocean?

B Read the title of the story. Look at the picture again. Answer the questions.

1. What do you think this story is about?

2. Can you guess what happens?

The Bottle

In 1979, Dorothy and John Peckham, a Los Angeles couple, went to Hawaii on vacation. They traveled by ship.

Some people on the ship were throwing bottles into the ocean. Each bottle had a piece of paper in it. On each piece of paper were a name, an address, and a message: "If you find this bottle, write to us."

Mrs. Peckham wanted to throw a bottle into the ocean, too. She wrote her name and address on a piece of paper. She put the piece of paper and $1 into a bottle. She put a cap on the bottle and threw the bottle into the water.

Three years later and 9,000 miles (15,000 kilometers) away, Hoa Van Nguyen was on a boat, too. But Mr. Nguyen was not on vacation. He was a refugee from Vietnam. Mr. Nguyen, his brother, and 30 other people were going to Thailand in a small boat. The boat was in the Gulf of Thailand.

There wasn't any drinking water in the boat, and Hoa was thirsty. He saw a bottle in the sea. The bottle was floating near the boat. "What's in the bottle? Maybe it's drinking water," he thought. Hoa took the bottle out of the sea and opened it. There wasn't any water in the bottle. But there was a dollar bill and a piece of paper. A name and an address were on the paper. The name was Peckham. The address was in Los Angeles, California.

Hoa and his brother arrived at the refugee camp in Thailand. Hoa used the dollar to buy some stamps. Then he wrote a letter to Mrs. Peckham. "We received a floating mailbox by a bottle on the way from Vietnam to Thailand," Hoa wrote. "Now we send a letter to the boss, and we wish you will answer us."

Hoa's English was not perfect, but Mrs. Peckham understood it. She answered Hoa's letter. Hoa wrote another letter, and she answered it, too. For two years, Hoa and Mrs. Peckham wrote back and forth. When Hoa got married at the camp, the Peckhams congratulated him. When Hoa and his wife had a baby boy, the Peckhams sent them money. Finally, Hoa asked the Peckhams, "Will you help me and my family? We want to come to the United States."

In 1985, the Nguyen family—Hoa, his wife, their son, and Hoa's brother—arrived in Los Angeles. Dorothy and John Peckham were waiting for them at the airport. When the Nguyens and the Peckhams met, they all began to cry. Their tears were tears of happiness. A few months after the Nguyens came to the United States, Mrs. Nguyen had another baby—a baby girl. The Nguyens named their daughter Dorothy.

2 VOCABULARY

Complete the sentences with the words below.

back and forth	floating	refugee	tears

1. Hoa Van Nguyen couldn't stay in Vietnam because it was dangerous for him there. He went to Thailand as a _____refugee_____.

2. Hoa saw a bottle on top of the water. It was _____ _____ near the boat.

3. Hoa sent a lot of letters to Mrs. Peckham, and she sent a lot of letters to him. For two years, they wrote _____.

4. The Peckhams and the Nguyens cried at the airport. They cried _____ of happiness.

3 COMPREHENSION

FINDING INFORMATION

There are two correct ways to complete each sentence below and one incorrect way. Circle the letters of the two correct answers.

1. Dorothy and John Peckham
   a. went to Hawaii on vacation.
   b. traveled by ship.
   c. traveled first class.

2. Mrs. Peckham threw a bottle into the ocean. In the bottle, she put
   a. a coin for good luck.
   b. a piece of paper.
   c. a dollar.

3. When Hoa Van Nguyen found Mrs. Peckham's bottle,
   a. it was three years later.
   b. he was 29 years old.
   c. he was in a boat in the Gulf of Thailand.

4. When Hoa arrived at the refugee camp in Thailand, he
   a. bought some stamps.
   b. wrote a letter to Mrs. Peckham.
   c. slept for 13 hours.

5. At the refugee camp, Hoa
   a. got married.
   b. learned English.
   c. became the father of a boy.

6. When the Nguyens arrived in Los Angeles,
   a. the Peckhams were waiting for them.
   b. the Nguyens and the Peckhams cried.
   c. it was 2 a.m.

UNDERSTANDING A SUMMARY

Imagine this: You want to tell the story "The Bottle" to a friend. You want to tell the story quickly, in only four sentences. Which four sentences tell the story best? Check (✓) your answer.

☐ 1. Dorothy Peckham wrote her name and address on a piece of paper, put the paper into a bottle, and threw the bottle into the ocean. The bottle floated to the Gulf of Thailand, 9,000 miles away. Hoa Van Nguyen, a refugee from Vietnam, found the bottle. He opened it because he was thirsty and thought, "Maybe there's drinking water in this bottle."

☐ 2. Dorothy Peckham wrote her name and address on a piece of paper, put the paper into a bottle, and threw the bottle into the ocean. The bottle floated to the Gulf of Thailand, 9,000 miles away. Hoa Van Nguyen, a refugee from Vietnam, found the bottle and wrote to Mrs. Peckham. She helped Mr. Nguyen and his family come to the United States.

UNDERSTANDING WORD GROUPS

Read each group of words. One word or phrase in each group doesn't belong. Find it and cross it out.

letter	Vietnam	in 1979	boss
stamps	Thailand	~~at the airport~~	son
mailbox	Los Angeles	in 1985	daughter
~~refugee~~	United States	three months later	brother

4 DISCUSSION

A The dotted line on the map shows the way the Nguyens came to the United States. On the same map, draw the way you came to the United States.

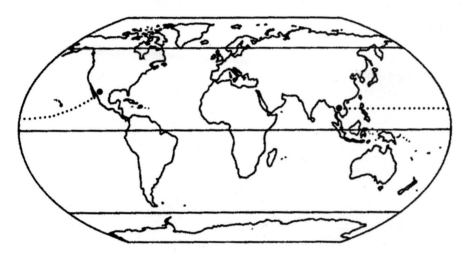

B Show your map to a partner. Tell your partner about your trip to the United States.

5 WRITING

Are you living in the United States? Read about the Nguyens' trip to the United States. Then write about your trip on your own paper.

1. The Nguyens came to the United States because they didn't like the government in Vietnam. Why did you come to the United States?

   I came to the United States because . . .

2. The Nguyens came to the United States on April 23, 1985. When did you come?

3. The Nguyens came by airplane. How did you come?

4. The Nguyens' trip was 15 hours long. How long was your trip?

5. The Nguyens arrived in Los Angeles. Where did you arrive?

6. The Nguyens felt tired but happy. How did you feel?

UNIT 21

1 PRE-READING

A Look at the picture. Answer the questions.

1. Does a waiter or waitress have a difficult job?

2. What makes a good waiter or waitress? If you are a customer? If you are the restaurant manager?

B Read the title of the story. Look at the picture again. Answer the questions.

1. What do you think this story is about?

2. Can you guess what happens?

The Last Laugh

Jodee Berry was a waitress at a big restaurant in Florida. One day, the restaurant's manager told the waitresses he had exciting news. "In May, we're going to have a contest at the restaurant," he said. "The waitress who sells the most food and drinks will win a new Toyota. So try to sell a lot of food and a lot of drinks during the month of May."

"Are you serious?" the waitresses asked the manager. "The top waitress will get a car?"

"A new Toyota," the manager repeated. "So work really hard in May. At the end of the month, one of you will have a new Toyota."

Jodee was excited about the contest. She was a good waitress and a hard worker. "I can win that contest," she thought.

During the month of May, Jodee worked extra hard. She sold a lot of food and drinks. At the end of the month, the manager announced the winner of the contest. It was Jodee! Jodee was very excited. "Now I'll get my new Toyota," she thought.

The manager covered Jodee's eyes with a blindfold and led her to the restaurant's parking lot. Then he uncovered her eyes. Jodee looked around the parking lot. She didn't see a new Toyota.

"Where's my Toyota?" she asked the manager.

The manager gave Jodee a box. "Here it is!" the manager said. "Here's your new toy Yoda!" The manager laughed.

At first, Jodee didn't understand. She looked at the box. Inside the box, there was a green doll. It was Yoda, a character from the *Star Wars* movies.

"Get it?" the manager asked. "It's a joke. You thought I said, 'Toyota.' But I said, 'Toy Yoda.' So here it is: your new toy Yoda." The manager laughed again.

Jodee didn't laugh. She was furious.

The next week, Jodee quit her job at the restaurant. Then she went to court. She told a judge her story. The manager told the judge his story, too. The judge listened to both stories and made a decision: The manager had to buy Jodee a new car.

"Go to a Toyota dealer," the judge told Jodee, "and pick out a new Toyota. The manager will pay for it."

"Any Toyota?" Jodee asked the judge.

"Any Toyota," the judge answered.

The next day, Jodee was driving a shiny new Toyota. Now it was her turn to laugh.

2 VOCABULARY

Which words have the same meaning as the words in *italics*? Write the letter of the answer on the line.

_b_ 1. The manager *repeated*, "A new Toyota."

____ 2. Jodee was the *top* waitress.

____ 3. "*Get it?*" the manager asked. "It's a joke."

____ 4. Jodee was *furious*.

____ 5. She *quit her job* at the restaurant.

a. very angry

b. said again

c. stopped working

d. best

e. Do you understand?

3 PRACTICING PRONUNCIATION

The underlined words are in the story. If you can say them correctly, you can say the words below them correctly, too. Practice with your teacher.

had	will	new	get	repeat	lot	drink
bad	bill	blew	let	beat	hot	blink
dad	fill	flew	met	heat	not	pink
mad	hill	grew	pet	neat	pot	sink
sad	Jill	stew	wet	seat	spot	stink

4 COMPREHENSION

REVIEWING THE STORY

Complete each sentence. Then read the story again and check your answers.

   Jodee Berry was a _____*waitress*_____ at a big restaurant. The manager said, "We're
   1.

going to have a _____ at the restaurant. The top waitress will
   2.

_____ a new Toyota."
   3.

   Jodee worked extra _____ and won the contest. But the manager
   4.

didn't give her a car. He gave her a green doll. It was Yoda, a character in the *Star*

Wars _____.
   5.

   Jodee went to court. The _____ decided that the manager had to buy
   6.

Jodee a new Toyota.

FINDING MORE INFORMATION

Read each sentence on the left. Which sentence on the right gives you more information? Write the letter of the answer on the line.

1. The manager had exciting news. _*d*_   a. She sold a lot of food and drinks.

2. Jodee worked extra hard. _____   b. It was Jodee.

3. The manager announced the winner of the   c. The manager had to buy Jodee a new car.
   contest. _____
                                                 d. He said, "We're going to have a contest
4. Inside the box, there was a green doll. _____   at the restaurant."

5. The judge made a decision. _____   e. It was Yoda, a character from the *Star Wars* movies.

5 WRITING/DISCUSSION

Jodee was a waitress. What about you? What kind of work do you do?

A In the spaces below, draw three pictures. In the first space, draw the work you did in your native country. In the second space, draw the work you do now. In the third space, draw the work you want to do.

my work before

my work now

the work I want

B Look at your drawings. Complete the sentences.

1. In my country, I worked as a/an _____ .

2. Now I work as a/an _____ .

3. I want to work as a/an _____ .

C Share your drawings and your sentences with the class.

UNIT 22

American veteran soldiers from World War II with Chi Hsii

1 PRE-READING

A Look at the picture. Answer the questions.

1. Chi Hsii was born in China. Why do you think he is with these men?

2. Chi Hsii now lives in the United States. How do you think he came to the United States?

B Read the title of the story. Look at the picture again. Answer the questions.

1. What do you think this story is about?

2. Can you guess what happens?

Old Friends

Chi Hsii, an 11-year-old boy, hurried along the road from his village in China. He carried a basket of eggs.

U.S. soldiers were at a camp near the boy's village. They were standing around a fire. When they saw the Chinese boy, they said, "Here comes breakfast."

It was November 1945. World War II was over. There was no more fighting. But there wasn't much food in China. Every day the Chinese boy brought some eggs to the U.S. soldiers. The soldiers took the eggs and gave the boy canned food. The soldiers were happy; they had fresh eggs. And the boy was happy; he had canned food.

Day after day, the Chinese boy traded food with the soldiers. The Chinese boy liked the soldiers, and the soldiers liked the Chinese boy. But there was a problem. The American soldiers couldn't say the boy's name. They tried and they tried, but they couldn't say "Chi Hsii." "Chi Hsii" sounds a little like the English words "two shoes." So, the soldiers called the boy "Charlie Two Shoes."

One day Charlie's father came with Charlie to the soldiers' camp. "We don't have enough food in our village," he said. "Please take my son. Take good care of him." For the next three years, Charlie Two Shoes lived with the American soldiers in their camp. He ate with the soldiers and dressed like the soldiers. He learned to read and write English at an American school.

In 1949, the soldiers left China. They flew back to the United States. They couldn't take Charlie with them. From the windows of the airplane, the soldiers looked at Charlie. Charlie was crying. The soldiers were crying, too.

After the soldiers left, they often thought about Charlie. They were afraid that Charlie was dead. Then, in 1980, they got a letter from Charlie. Charlie was alive! He wanted to come to the United States.

The soldiers sent Charlie a plane ticket. Charlie came to the United States and lived with one of the soldiers. Later, the soldiers bought plane tickets for Charlie's wife and three children, too. They also gave Charlie $5,000 to open a Chinese restaurant.

Sometimes people ask the soldiers, "Why did you give Charlie so much help?" The soldiers answer, "We were unhappy in China; we were cold and lonely. Then came Charlie. He was always smiling, always happy. When Charlie was with us, we felt happy. Yes, we gave a lot to Charlie. But Charlie gave a lot to us, too."

2 VOCABULARY

Complete the sentences with the words below.

camp   hurried   over   traded   village

1. The soldiers were waiting for Charlie, so he walked fast. He _____*hurried*_____ along the road.

2. The soldiers' houses had no bathrooms, kitchens, or heat. The soldiers built fires to keep warm. They cooked over the fires, too. The soldiers lived in a _____.

3. Chi Hsii's town in China was very small. He lived in a _____.

4. In November 1945, the fighting was finished. World War II was _____.

5. The Chinese boy gave the soldiers eggs, and the soldiers gave the boy canned food. The Chinese boy _____ food with the soldiers.

3 COMPREHENSION

REMEMBERING DETAILS

One word in each sentence is not correct. Find the word and cross it out. Write the correct word.

1. Chi Hsii was a ~~French~~ *Chinese* boy.

2. U.S. doctors were at a camp near the boy's village.

3. World War I was over.

4. Every day the Chinese boy brought some fruit to the U.S. soldiers.

5. Chi Hsii sounds a little like the Spanish words "two shoes."

6. For the next three days, Charlie Two Shoes lived with the American soldiers in their camp.

7. In 1949, the soldiers flew back to England.

8. After the soldiers left, they never thought about Charlie.

UNDERSTANDING CAUSE AND EFFECT

Find the best way to complete each sentence. Write the letter of the answer on the line.

1. When the soldiers saw the Chinese boy, they said, "Here comes breakfast" __b__

2. The American soldiers called the boy "Charlie Two Shoes" _____

3. All the soldiers were sad _____

4. The soldiers gave a lot to Charlie _____

a. because they couldn't say "Chi Hsii."

b. because he brought them eggs every day.

c. because Charlie gave a lot to them.

d. because they couldn't take Charlie with them to the United States.

UNDERSTANDING A SUMMARY

Imagine this: You want to tell the story "Old Friends" to your friend. You want to tell the story quickly, in only four sentences. Which four sentences tell the story best? Check (✓) your answer.

☐ 1. After World War II, a Chinese boy lived with U.S. soldiers in their camp in China. The soldiers called the boy "Charlie Two Shoes" because they couldn't say his Chinese name. When the soldiers went back to the United States, they couldn't take Charlie with them. Thirty-one years later, the soldiers helped Charlie and his family come to the United States.

☐ 2. After World War II, there were U.S. soldiers in China. Some soldiers lived in a camp near a Chinese village. Every day a Chinese boy from the village brought eggs to the U.S. soldiers, and the soldiers gave the boy canned food. The soldiers were happy because they had fresh eggs, and the boy was happy because he had canned food.

4 WRITING/DISCUSSION

Charlie opened a Chinese restaurant in the United States with the money the soldiers gave him.

A Imagine this: Someone gives your class money to open an international restaurant. What dish from your country will be on the menu? Draw a picture of the dish in the space below.

B Answer the questions below about your dish. Write your answers on the lines.

1. What is the name of the dish? _____

2. What is it made of? _____

3. Who makes this dish in your family? _____

4. When do you eat it? (For example, "We eat it in the summer" or "We eat it only on holidays.")

   _____

C Show your picture to a partner. Tell your partner about the dish from your native country.

D Charlie and the soldiers were old friends. Complete the sentences below about an old friend of yours. Then tell your partner about your old friend.

1. My friend's name is _____ .

2. I met my friend in _____ .

3. My friend lives in _____ .

4. He / She is _____ .

5. Together we _____ .

6. I like my friend because _____ .

ANSWER KEY

VOCABULARY   page 3

   2. a   **3.** b   **4.** b   **5.** c

REMEMBERING DETAILS   page 4

   2. ~~ticket~~ / sample

   3. ~~orange~~ / lemon

   4. ~~eat~~ / try

   5. ~~bananas~~ / lemons

   6. ~~dishes~~ / salad

   7. ~~fine~~ / sick

   8. ~~soup~~ / soap

   9. ~~coffee~~ / tea

UNDERSTANDING CAUSE AND EFFECT   page 4

   2. c   **3.** b   **4.** a

UNDERSTANDING A SUMMARY   page 4

   2

WRITING   page 5

In his mailbox, he found a free sample of dish soap. The dish soap had a little lemon juice in it.

   Joe looked at his bottle of soap. There was a picture of two lemons on the label. Over the lemons were the words "with Real Lemon Juice."

   Joe thought the soap was lemon juice. He put it on his salad and ate it. After he ate the salad, he felt sick. Poor Joe!

UNIT **2**

VOCABULARY   page 7

   2. a   **3.** c   **4.** b

LOOKING FOR DETAILS   page 8

A potatoes, fried vegetables, meat, dessert, sandwiches, cake

B baked beans on toast, fish, vegetables

REVIEWING THE STORY page 8

2. seat
3. back
4. die
5. diet
6. weight
7. woman
8. stop
9. pounds
10. married

UNDERSTANDING CAUSE AND EFFECT page 8

2. d 3. a 4. b 5. e

UNIT 3

VOCABULARY page 11

2. e 3. c 4. a 5. d

REMEMBERING DETAILS page 12

2. nursing home
3. police officers drove to Torggate Street
4. one kilometer away
5. address
6. minutes
7. 94 years old
8. twice a week

UNDERSTANDING DIALOGUE page 13

2. e 3. b 4. a 5. d

UNIT 4

VOCABULARY page 15

2. ready
3. can't believe it
4. delivered
5. altogether

UNDERSTANDING WORD GROUPS page 16

labels   soccer   doctor

REMEMBERING DETAILS page 16

2. ~~p.m.~~ / a.m.
3. ~~morning~~ / weekend
4. ~~schools~~ / restaurants
5. ~~write~~ / marry
6. ~~postcards~~ / letters
7. ~~70~~ / 700
8. ~~wrote~~ / delivered

UNDERSTANDING QUOTATIONS page 16

2. d   3. b   4. a

UNIT 5

VOCABULARY page 19

2. broke into
3. stolen
4. delivered
5. cash

UNDERSTANDING THE MAIN IDEAS page 20

2. a   3. b   4. b   5. a

REMEMBERING DETAILS pages 20–21

~~truck~~ / car
~~dirty~~ / broken
~~back~~ / front
~~purse~~ / wallet
~~hamburger~~ / pizza
~~Wednesday~~ / Monday
~~woman~~ / man

UNIT 6

VOCABULARY page 23

2. adopted
3. found out
4. exactly
5. guessed

UNDERSTANDING THE MAIN IDEAS page 24

1. b   2. a   3. c

LOOKING FOR DETAILS page 24

color eyes
smile
dark, curly hair
birthday

UNDERSTANDING CAUSE AND EFFECT page 24

2. a   **3.** b   **4.** c   **5.** d

UNIT 7

VOCABULARY page 27

2. packed up
3. about
4. pass
5. give up

REMEMBERING DETAILS page 28

2. car
3. difficult
4. emergency
5. Reading
6. 950
7. passed the test
8. car
9. drives

ORGANIZING INFORMATION page 28

What she does now	What she doesn't do now
She picks vegetables.	She doesn't get on a bus.
She sells vegetables.	She doesn't ride the bus to the market.

FINDING MORE INFORMATION page 29

2. g   **3.** d   **4.** f   **5.** c   **6.** e   **7.** a

UNIT 8

VOCABULARY page 31

2. lonely
3. simple
4. grave
5. ground

REMEMBERING DETAILS   page 32

2. ~~Sammy~~ / Bobby
3. ~~1958~~ / 1858
4. ~~Ireland~~ / Scotland
5. ~~four~~ / fourteen
6. ~~large~~ / small
7. ~~man~~ / dog

REVIEWING THE STORY   page 32

2. fire
3. hungry
4. lonely
5. rainy
6. weather
7. years

UNIT 9

VOCABULARY   page 35

2. missing
3. notice
4. coughed
5. throat

UNDERSTANDING THE MAIN IDEAS   page 36

1. a   2. c

REMEMBERING DETAILS   page 36

2. ~~pie~~ / cake
3. ~~spoons~~ / coins
4. ~~breakfast~~ / dinner
5. ~~floor~~ / table
6. ~~sixth~~ / fourth
7. ~~days~~ / years
8. ~~cake~~ / coin

UNDERSTANDING A SUMMARY   page 36

2

UNIT **10**

VOCABULARY page 39

2. almost
3. cast
4. rent
5. got caught

UNDERSTANDING WORD GROUPS page 40

shopping   pizza   perfectly

REVIEWING THE STORY page 40

2. dance
3. leg
4. cast
5. bandage
6. wheelchair
7. without
8. girlfriend

UNDERSTANDING TIME RELATIONSHIPS page 40

2. d   3. e   4. a   5. b

UNIT **11**

VOCABULARY page 43

2. awake
3. recognized
4. froze
5. worse

UNDERSTANDING CAUSE AND EFFECT page 44

2. a   3. e   4. c   5. b

REMEMBERING INFORMATION page 44

2. a   3. b, c   4. c   5. b

UNIT **12**

VOCABULARY page 47

2. cashier
3. counter
4. lottery ticket
5. won

UNDERSTANDING WORD GROUPS page 48

potatoes   diet   sick

REMEMBERING DETAILS page 48

2. ~~movie~~ / lottery
3. ~~floor~~ / counter
4. ~~money~~ / tickets
5. ~~$5~~ / $50,000
6. ~~anger~~ / shock
7. ~~uncle~~ / mother
8. ~~friendly~~ / honest

UNDERSTANDING CAUSE AND EFFECT page 48

2. d   3. a   4. b

UNIT 13

VOCABULARY page 51

2. a   3. b   4. a

UNDERSTANDING THE MAIN IDEAS page 52

2. b   3. b   4. b   5. a   6. a

UNDERSTANDING A SUMMARY page 52

1

UNIT 14

VOCABULARY page 55

2. a   3. a   4. b

FINDING INFORMATION page 56

2. b, c
3. a, b
4. a, c
5. b, c

MAKING CONNECTIONS page 56

2. a   3. d   4. c

REMEMBERING DETAILS page 57

2. ~~California~~ / Florida
3. ~~daughters~~ / sons
4. ~~ten~~ / two
5. ~~beach~~ / highway

UNIT **15**

VOCABULARY page 59

2. trouble
3. shouted
4. plenty

REMEMBERING DETAILS page 60

~~July~~ / June
~~family~~ / friends
~~Peru~~ / Colombia
~~rainstorm~~ / snowstorm
~~pocket~~ / backpack
~~radio~~ / cell phone
~~hours~~ / minutes
~~man~~ / woman
~~ski~~ / rescue

UNDERSTANDING DIALOGUE page 60

lost
minutes
help
Stay

FINDING MORE INFORMATION page 61

2. a   3. e   4. b   5. d

UNIT **16**

VOCABULARY page 63

2. a   3. b   4. a

FINDING INFORMATION page 64

2. a, b
3. b, c
4. b, c
5. b, c

UNDERSTANDING CAUSE AND EFFECT page 64

2. d   3. a   4. c

LOOKING FOR DETAILS pages 64–65

A his job
the weather
the food
the water

B American sports
American food

UNIT **17**

VOCABULARY page 67
2. wedding
3. guests
4. whispered
5. changed his mind

UNDERSTANDING THE MAIN IDEAS page 68
2. c   3. c   4. a

UNDERSTANDING QUOTATIONS page 68
2. c   3. d   4. a

UNIT **18**

VOCABULARY page 71
2. b   3. a   4. a

FINDING INFORMATION page 72
2. Jimmy and his father were playing on a Chicago beach.
3. Jimmy ran onto the ice.
4. The ice broke.
5. Firefighters pulled Jimmy out of the water.
6. Jimmy was in the water for over twenty minutes.

UNDERSTANDING CAUSE AND EFFECT page 72
2. e   3. a   4. b   5. c

UNDERSTANDING WORD GROUPS page 72
pilot   nervous   garden

UNIT 19

VOCABULARY   page 75
2. army
3. exploded
4. happened
5. medal
6. hero

UNDERSTANDING WORD GROUPS   page 76
letter   school   excited

FINDING INFORMATION   page 76
2. eight years
3. to the Olympics
4. the Hungarian team
5. the gold medal in pistol shooting
6. In 1952

UNDERSTANDING SEQUENCE   page 77
1939   He won the Hungarian National Pistol-Shooting Competition.
1940–1948   He practiced for the Olympics.
1948   He won his first Olympic gold medal.
1952   He won his second Olympic gold medal.

UNIT 20

VOCABULARY   page 79
2. floating
3. back and forth
4. tears

FINDING INFORMATION   page 80
2. b, c
3. a, c
4. a, b
5. a, c
6. a, b

UNDERSTANDING A SUMMARY   page 80
2

UNDERSTANDING WORD GROUPS   page 81
Los Angeles   at the airport   boss

UNIT 21

VOCABULARY   page 83

2. d   3. e   4. a   5. c

REVIEWING THE STORY   page 84

2. contest
3. win
4. hard
5. movies
6. judge

FINDING MORE INFORMATION   page 84

2. a   3. b   4. e   5. c

UNIT 22

VOCABULARY   page 87

2. camp
3. village
4. over
5. traded

REMEMBERING DETAILS   page 88

2. ~~doctors~~ / soldiers
3. ~~I~~ / II
4. ~~fruit~~ / eggs
5. ~~Spanish~~ / English
6. ~~days~~ / years
7. ~~England~~ / the United States
8. ~~never~~ / often

UNDERSTANDING CAUSE AND EFFECT   page 88

2. a   3. d   4. c

UNDERSTANDING A SUMMARY   page 88

1

CREDITS